PHILANTHROPY IN THE HISTORY
OF AMERICAN HIGHER EDUCATION

PHILANTHROPY IN THE HISTORY OF AMERICAN HIGHER EDUCATION

Jesse Brundage Sears

with a New Introduction by
Roger L. Geiger

Transaction Publishers
New Brunswick (U.S.A.) and London (U.K.)

Library of Congress Catalog Number: 89-35089
ISBN: 0-88738-314-9
Printed in the United States of America

Library of Congress Cataloging-in-Publication Data

Sears, Jesse Brundage.
    Philanthropy in the history of American higher education / by Jesse Brundage
Sears; with a new introduction by Roger L. Geiger.
        p. cm. — (Philanthropy and society)
    Reprint. Originally published: Washington: G.P.O., 1922.
    Includes bibliographical references and index.
    ISBN 0-88738-314-9
    1. Endowments — United States. 2. Education, Higher — United States —
History. 3. Universities and colleges — United States — History. I. Title. II.
Series.
LB2336.S43   1989
378.73 — dc20   89-35089
                                                                              CIP

CONTENTS.

INTRODUCTION TO THE TRANSACTION EDITION

Roger L. Geiger

Jesse B. Sears's doctoral dissertation on the role of philanthropy in the development of American higher education, written in 1918 and subsequently published by the U.S. Bureau of Education, stands as the first systematic study of this subject. That it can be read with interest and profit some two generations later, despite its limitations, is tribute to the diligence and the quality of mind that its author brought to the task of exploring an uncharted subject.

The novelty of his topic led him to grope among such writers as Turgot, Adam Smith, and John Stuart Mill for some theoretical guidance. Finding little help, he took refuge in empiricism. Rummaging through a wide collection of college histories, university annual reports, and reports from the commissioner of education, Sears compiled a broad array of data that were indicative of the dimensions of philanthropy in the development of American higher education. These data were presented in some forty tables, in part "to make them fully available for future use in more intensive studies". Also characteristic of Sears's empiricism was the breadth of his coverage—from the great universities to the manual-labor colleges. In both these respects, his study differed from its sequel, *Philanthropy in the Shaping of American Higher Education* by Merle Curti and Roderick Nash. Those authors dismiss Sears's study as "largely quantitative,"[1] but they might be faulted themselves for producing a largely anecdotal coverage of an inherently measurable phenomenon. There is no actual need, however, to choose between these two works. If Sears's data and broad coverage establish the centrality of philanthropy to the development of higher education in the United States, the narrative and interpretation provided by Curti and Nash permit a somewhat deeper consideration of the significance of this fact. Sears's pioneering effort thus still endures as a complement to the literature on this topic.

JESSE BRUNDAGE SEARS.

It is something of an oddity that someone from rural Missouri, who did not lay eyes upon a university until his twenty-ninth year, should become the chronicler of higher education philanthropy.[2] This occurred more as a result of academic circumstance than personal inclination. Jesse Sears's true calling lay with public schools, and his career stretched from the era of the one-room rural school to that of modern municipal school systems.

Sears grew up on a none-too-prosperous farm in rural Missouri together with six siblings. His parents instilled in him a strong ambition to better himself but had neither the resources nor the worldly knowledge to provide young Jesse with much assistance. Very slowly, Sears found his own way. At the age when most young men would enter college, Jesse started high school in Kidder, Missouri. After less than two years there, he received and accepted an offer to teach school in a nearby rural district. The two years he spent presiding over a one-room school were fulfilling and seem to have oriented Sears toward pursuing a career in education. First, however, he had to spend another two years back in Kidder earning a high-school degree. After graduation he taught for one year and then made a leap to being superintendent of another rural school district. The following year brought a further advancement—to the principalship of a larger, "graded" school. Still, Sears was deeply aware of the deficiencies of his own knowledge, the provincialism of his milieu, and the limitations that these factors placed upon his aspirations for professional success. Nearly thirty years of age, and now married, Sears resolved to go to college.

In the summer of 1906, Jesse and his wife, with fifty dollars in savings and a promise of financial help from his brother-in-law, left Missouri for Stanford University. The financial assistance never materialized; however, arriving only months after the great San Francisco earthquake, Sears was able to earn extra money by cleaning mortar from the bricks of crumbled buildings. He was admitted to the university despite a deficient high-school record largely because of his maturity and earnestness. He quickly gravitated toward education and was taken under wing by Ellwood P. Cubberley, who would persist as guide and colleague throughout Sears's academic career.

Cubberley was a giant in the establishment of education as a field of professional study; he was also the individual most responsible for developing the Stanford School of Education where Sears spent his entire career. Cubberley not only built up the department as its head but upon his retirement donated the funds for the building in which it is still housed.[3] Cubberley had come to Stanford just eight years before Sears, in 1898, as a virtual neophyte to the field. He had begun his career as a teacher, advanced to the presidency of Vincennes University, and for the prior two years had been superintendent of schools in San Diego. Now, as the new head of the Department of Education, he was told by President David Starr Jordan that he would have three years to make his field into a respectable university subject, or it would be dropped from the curriculum. Above all, this meant establishing traditions of academic research and writing.

Cubberley attacked this task with characteristic zeal. Having little material on which to base the professional study of education, he endeavored to do what was needed himself in order to build a body of academic knowledge. Cubberley first sought to educate himself at the only place in the country where educational scholarship was then cultivated — Columbia University Teachers College. For his Master's degree (1902), he focused upon the history of education — "the one area of educational research which at the time possessed a thoroughgoing, scholarly method of inquiry."[4] His doctorate at Teachers College (1905) took him into the area of school administration, the area in which he would do most of his subsequent writing. One of his most important contributions was pioneering the methodology for systematic school surveys. Cubberley also sought to bring the findings of science to bear upon the problems of education by editing a series of basic texts. In thirty years, he wrote and (mostly) edited 103 volumes in this series alone. Despite a copious personal output, Cubberley was a generalist rather than a true scholar. He possessed a broad grasp and sure instincts toward his field. In his series and as department head at Stanford he relied on others for more specialized expertise. In 1910 he brought Lewis B. Terman to the department, who would become one of the country's foremost educational psychologists. The following year, after an intensive apprenticeship, Jesse Sears rejoined the department as a full faculty member.

Sears had begun working as Cubberley's assistant in his second undergraduate year, a post that he continued to hold until graduation (1909). At this juncture Sears seems to have been identified as Cubberley's protege, and it was virtually understood that he would have a place in the Stanford department. Specifically, he was earmarked to take over the history of education from Cubberley. This subject was not Cubberley's specialty, even though he would subsequently write one of the best-known surveys in this field. For later generations, Cubberley came to represent the epitome of Whig historiography in American education. The historical evolution of education represented the progressive realization of democracy and freedom for Cubberley, with the development of free public education representing the *summum bonum*.[5]

Sears would later defend the historical writings of his mentor, but he did not exactly emulate him. Cubberley's history, according to Sears, addressed the overriding themes that he perceived in the past — particularly the growth of democracy and the idea of free public schools. Other events and institutions were only included to the extent that they contributed to these larger developments. Sears admitted that Cubberley was perhaps

too quick to seize upon these major trends, and that as a consequence he neglected other aspects of the past.[6]
    There is nevertheless a certain Cubberleyesque element in Sears's own history of higher education philanthropy. The key trend on which he seized was the significance of philanthropy for the overall development of higher education. The "test" employed for gauging its beneficence is service to society (p. 109). It will be argued that Sears may well have missed some of the more significant implications of philanthropy in his day, largely due to his closeness to events. In any case, he seems to have had a far more empirical temperament than his mentor. Sears speaks of his own education in terms of the "thousands of new facts needed in [his] studies" (p. 41); of finding his way "among great masses of facts" (p. 47); and his approach was no different in his history. This was taken to be the scientific approach to writing history of his day.
    Immediately following his graduation, Cubberley helped to arrange an instructorship for Sears in the history of education at the University of Wisconsin. One year of teaching and study there was followed by a summer session at the University of Chicago and then a year of full-time graduate work in the Ph.D. program at Teachers College. Here Sears studied the history of education with Paul Monroe, as had Cubberley. It was Monroe who steered him to the subject of philanthropy.
    During a long and distinguished career at Teachers College, Monroe wrote extensively on the history of education, contributed substantially to the historiography of American education through the direction of numerous doctoral theses, and was chief editor for a five-volume *Cyclopedia of Education* (1911–13), which was for long a landmark in the field. The Monroe School of educational historians, who were contemporaries of Sears, generally elaborated the prevailing view that "the history of American education is the history of the public school realizing itself over time."[7] Monroe himself, whose own canvas was worldwide, proffered an evolutionary perspective that rationalized this development. The first stage of the development of education was one in which schools were supported by "private voluntary enterprise, from motives of religious or philanthropic character." This phase was superceded as states gradually accepted "the responsibility for general education of all the people as one of the functions of government."[8] In light of this work, Jesse Sears appears to have been out of step with his classmates in undertaking a topic in higher education and in choosing to emphasize the current, rather than the past, importance of private voluntary support. The topic actually emerged from Monroe's *Cyclopedia*, which he was in the process of compiling during Sears's year at Teachers College.
    In his own writings, Monroe fully recognized the continuing importance of philanthropy for American higher education. Judging from the contributions to related topics in his *Cyclopedia*, he probably could turn to no established scholar to address this issue.[9] Under these circumstances, Monroe suggested this topic to Sears. In 1911 Sears completed his preliminary exams for his doctorate and commenced gathering data for his dissertation. This early canvas of the subject became the basis for his contribution to Monroe's *Cyclopedia*, "Philanthropy, Educational," which appeared in Volume IV (1913).[10]
    Just five years after beginning college, Jesse Sears returned to Stanford to assume an instructorship in Cubberley's Department of Education. There he soon became frustrated with teaching the history of education. Despite his studies at Teachers College, he lacked an adequate background in history or foreign languages for doing further work in this field. His interests and his writings gravitated toward the problems of current public school systems, and he concluded that history was not his calling. In 1916, Cubberley's own interest in history revived as he began preparing *Public Education in the United States* (1918), and he relieved Sears of the burden of the history course. But Jesse still had the requirement of his dissertation hanging over his head. He returned to Teachers College in 1918, buckled down, and wrote *Philanthropy in the History of American Higher Education* to fulfill the Ph.D. requirements. This appears to be the end of Sears's interest in the subject.[11] By this juncture he had found a far more congenial outlet for his professional activities—the "school survey." These instruments were regarded in the

parlance of the day as "a tool... of educational engineering," intended to evaluate scientifically the efficiency of schools.[12] Sears took part in his first school survey in 1915 together with Cubberley. In 1925 he published the definitive guide to this procedure, and many additional opportunities for surveys naturally ensured. Most of the remainder of Sears' career was devoted to the task of improving public school systems through this means.

SEARS'S *PHILANTHROPY.*

When Sears sought theoretical guidelines for his subject, his only recourse was to writings concerned with endowments, a literature that was particularly concerned with the baleful effects of the "dead hand." The French *philosophe* Turgot had written of the numerous and often bizarre accretions of permanent foundations that existed in France at the end of ancièn régime. He charged that none of those endowments could meet the test of "enlightened policy." Instead, Turgot advocated the standard of "public utility" in judging the uses to which such funds were devoted. In England the liberal economists were no less hostile to the effects of permanent endowments. They had before them examples of decadence in the richly endowed colleges of Oxford and Cambridge. According to Adam Smith, it was precisely their wealth that insulated them from the salutory influence of the marketplace. Sears had to move forward in time to the mid-nineteenth century in order to find a defender of endowments. John Stuart Mill argued, somewhat weakly, that the "inconvenience" of such trusts ought to be tolerated as an inseparable part of guaranteeing human freedom, minority rights, and private property (p. 6). From all this, Sears gleaned a scant justification for philanthropy: that it should be permitted in education, under public supervision, largely because it promoted what would today be styled *diversity.*

Sears clearly perceived that the foregoing discussion about the perpetuation of superannuated privilege had little to do with the practical difficulties of establishing colleges in the American colonies. There philanthropy played an indispensable role in supplying the resources that made the colonial colleges possible in the first place. Indeed, after describing the connection between strategically important gifts and the founding of these colleges, he concluded that "philanthropy is clearly the mother of the colonial colleges" (p. 16). The continued involvement of philanthropy in nurturing these progeny was somewhat more complicated.

Sears made a determined effort to piece together the financial circumstances of the colonial colleges from fragmentary evidence. He stopped short, perhaps wisely in light of his limited sources, of presenting the kind of comprehensive picture of college finances that Margery Foster was later to piece together for seventeenth-century Harvard.[13] Sears's data are nevertheless sufficient to establish some important truths about the colonial colleges. First, although they were quasi-public institutions,[14] only in Virginia, New York, and Connecticut did grants from the colonies outweigh gifts from individuals as a source of income. Second, revenues from students were inadequte to support even the basic operations of these colleges. Supplemental revenues were thus an absolute necessity; and indeed, Sears's figures show most of the income from gifts being devoted to present use.

Nevertheless, the paramount role of philanthropy was in providing the capital that made institutional development possible. The first requirement of a permanent institutions was the erection of a college building to house both students and tutors. The migration and fragmentation of the Collegiate School of Connecticut in the years before the gift of Elihu Yale secured it a permanent home in New Haven or the peregrinations of the College of New Jersey before it settled in Princeton, well illustrate the impermanence of a propertyless institution. Beyond this, gifts provided the extra capital that allowed these rudimentary schools to evolve into places of learning. College libraries grew predominately from the accretion of donations but more significant were the gifts that provided for the establishment of professorships. Teaching in the colonial colleges was confided predominantly to tutors—themselves recent graduates of the college preparing for the ministry—and in small part by the president. The gifts of Thomas Hollis that created the first professorships at Harvard, in divinity (1721) and natural Philosophy (1727), added a new element—support for learned individuals to both teach and contribute to their field.

Sears concluded that giving to the colonial colleges furthered the fundamental purposes of those institutions rather than imposing unwanted obligations (p. 31). This view seems consistent with the conditions of philanthropy in that era. Colonial society generated little surplus wealth. The small sums that were given locally to sustain the operations of the colleges came largely from a sympathetic community of coreligionists. Larger amounts were generally sought abroad, which allowed for limited involvement of the donor with the college. Neither Elihu Yale nor Thomas Hollis ever laid eyes upon the institutions they assisted. Over time, the ubiquitous needs of the colleges and the generosity of individuals in the Mother Country led to highly organized fund-raising efforts.[15] Under these circumstances, at great geographical distance, it was the donors more often than the colleges that had cause to complain about the uses to which gifts were put. The most successful fund-raising effort of the colonial period was launched by Eleazer Wheelock on behalf of his Charity School for Indians. His emissaries, especially a rare Indian preacher named Samson Occum, raised more than £10,000 in England for the purpose of educating and christianizing Indians. When Wheelock used these funds to found Dartmouth College, however, the mission of serving the Indians was quite rapidly eclipsed by that of operating a college of the conventional sort.[16] Sears does not seem to have considered the possibility of the donee manipulating the donors.

Conditions would change in the next period discussed by Sears, the ninety years from the Declaration of Independence to the end of the Civil War. This era witnessed the proliferation of colleges across the new nation but a paucity of public support for higher education. The impetus for the founding of colleges typically came from the competition of religious denominations and the zeal of local citizens to boost the standing of their fledgling communities.[17] This combination frequently produced the land and sufficient funds for launching a college, but the fees of students were seldom adequate to provide for satisfactory operations. With the exception of a handful of Eastern institutions, the colleges of the antebellum period were chronically underfunded.

American higher education between the Revolution and the Civil War was overwhelmingly supported by private funds—the fees that could be afforded by the none-too-affluent students and an intermittent flow of private philanthropy. To these sources of support, historian Frederick Rudolph has proposed to add the involuntary contributions of underpaid faculty.[18] Under the conditions of penury to which such circumstances gave rise, donors found themselves in an unusually strong position. Sears related the example of a potential donor to Oberlin, and one of dubious reliability, who was able to exact far-reaching concessions from the college board of trustees (p. 46). More typical and more pervasive was the considerable influence of organized religion over the colleges. The churches through their educational societies or through their organizational networks constituted one of the few conduits of philanthropic support for hard-pressed colleges.

Until the very end of this period, and then with possible exceptions only for Harvard and Yale, giving to higher education tended to be small in scale.[19] Significant amounts had to be accumulated through subscriptions or, as in the case of Yale in the early 1830s, organized drives. Even so, it was possible to fund some significant innovations, like seminaries for women or manual-labor colleges (pp. 44–47). The endowing of the scientific schools at Yale and Harvard, and earlier the founding of Rensselaer Polytechnic Institute, are exceptional cases of substantial individual philanthropy assisting or making possible significant departures from the established collegiate pattens. But this type of giving would characterize the subsequent period. After the Civil War, burgeoning private fortunes attained such magnitudes that individual acts of philanthropy could alter the nature of American higher education.

The passage of the Morrill Land-Grant Act in 1862 ushered in a new era for American higher education. State-sponsored colleges and universities were soon created where they had not existed before, and new life was breathed into the struggling state institutions already in existence. But for a generation after the Morrill Act, American higher education continued to be dominated by private institutions. In the generation following, a rapidly developing sector of public universities took its place beside an even more robust array of private ones.[20] Table 18 (p. 55), where Sears presents the sources of income for higher education, illustrates this seldom recognized situation. Not until after 1885 did all public funds for higher education exceed $1 million, and only near 1910 did these funds become the largest single source of higher education revenues. Before then, gifts appear more often than not to have been the main source. Philanthropy, then, played a large and consistent role in sustaining higher education through the nineteenth century.

Moreover, Sears also did some lengthy compilations in order to determine that, with the exception of the war years, education was the principal object of large-scale American philanthropy (p. 60). The average he calculates for education's share — 43 percent — compares with current figures of about 14 percent during the 1980s.[21] Sears concluded that this was a fairly dependable source of income for higher education, a statement that was true only in the aggregate. In fact, these gifts fell quite unevenly over American colleges and universities, and it was precisely this unevenness that caused the greatest impact of philanthropy — furthering the differentiation of institutional roles in American higher education.

The most salient result of philanthropy in the era following the Civil War was the founding of new kinds of institutions with large individual gifts. The magnitudes of these gifts, made possible by the growing fortunes in industrializing America, guaranteed that the innovations that were brought into existence would endure and usually prosper, thereby contributing directly to the diversification of American higher education. The college founded and supported by Matthew Vassar resolved the ambiguous state of women's education by placing it definitively on the collegiate level. Cornell University was the result of both public policy in the Morrill Act and private philanthropy, but the contribution of Ezra Cornell made it possible for that university to become the first outstanding success among land-grant institutions — an exemplar of a fully rounded university to other struggling schools of agriculture and engineering. And the bequest of Johns Hopkins, carefully implemented by its trustees, gave the United States a type of institution that had been lacking — a semi-Germanic, research-oriented university.

When historian Laurence Veysey considered the relationship between these single-donor universities and their founders, particularly the role of Jane Lathrop Stanford as sole trustee for Stanford University and the falling out of Jonas Clark and Clark University's imperious president, G. Stanley Hall, he emphasized the intrusions of donors into the institutions they had brought into being.[22] Sears, however, makes an opposite point. The considerable wealth of these institutions permitted them to resist the unwanted influence of potential donors (p. 70). In the long run, this has been the more important result. The strong financial underpinnings of these endowed universities have permitted them to chart their own courses.[23]

Philanthropy nevertheless did exert an influence over the courses that institutions chose to chart, but this occurred largely in a manner that eluded Sears's analysis. Together with the growing role of foundations, the most significant trend in giving to American higher education in the early twentieth century was the growing contributions of alumni. Furthermore, it was the oldest and the richest of universities, Harvard and Yale, that pioneered this development and reaped the greatest bounty. It was probably because of Sears's personal remoteness from these Eastern universities and the powerful traditions embodied in their undergraduate colleges that he failed to perceive the decisive role of alumni in both supporting and shaping these institutions. While at Teachers College he was, of course, across the street from Columbia, but even that Eastern university differed markedly from patterns of support that were emerging at Harvard, Yale, and Princeton.[24]

American colleges had historically turned to their alumni, among others, for gifts to meet their needs or aspirations. What changed at the beginning of the twentieth century was the spontaneous formation of almuni organizations for the collective provision of substantial and continual support. The Yale Alumni Fund was begun in 1890 as a means for contributors who were not rich to pool their modest contributions to alma mater. By World War I the fund itself had accumulated more than $1 million and was giving Yale more than $100,000 annually. At Harvard, regular alumni giving initially took the form of class gifts. In 1905, and every year thereafter, the class celebrating its twenty-fifth anniversary contributed a gift of at least $100,000 to the university. In the long run, alumni giving turned out to be the most dependable and the most lucrative source of voluntary support.[25]

At the time Sears was writing, Harvard had already emerged as the wealthiest American university, and smaller Yale was not far behind. During the next two decades, their gifts, largely from loyal alumni, far outdistanced those of other institutions.[26] This largesse produced two somewhat contradictory results: Their wealth allowed them to assemble the faculty and construct the facilities befitting great research universities, whereas the overriding influence of alumni caused them to pay utmost heed to the social composition and extracurricular side of the undergraduate college. With regard to the latter, the influence of the alumni constituency was diffuse but pervasive.[27]

Sears devoted his final substantive chapter to another philanthropic development of great contemporary importance, the involvement in higher education of the great foundations. Although the appearance of these institutions was clearly portentious, it was difficult at the time Sears was writing to perceive what their ultimate impact might be. The two behemoths of the foundation world—the Carnegie Corporation and the Rocke-feller Foundation—were founded respectively in 1911 and 1913. Their eventual role would not become apparent until the 1920s, when foundations in general began to operate under far more congenial conditions.[28] Prior to this, the Rockefeller trusts, in particular, were often accused of being fronts for the interests of the family. With these latter events undoubtedly in mind, Sears writes that the actions of the foundations would not go unsupervised (p. 102). Sears himself, however, may have lacked sufficient perspective to monitor and interpret this rapidly changing phenomenon.

The initial foundations of the nineteenth century, the Peabody and Slater funds, had a fundamentally different orientation from the twentieth-century creations of Carnegie and Rockefeller. The former were designed to aid the weakest elements of society, specifically to promote education in the "more destitute portions of the Southern and Southwestern States" (p. 82). Carnegie and Rockefeller, for the most part, dedicated their philanthropic activities to aiding mankind collectively through the advancement of knowledge or the improvement of education. Improving educational institutions, however, came to be interpreted in a somewhat Darwinian sense—providing additional assistance for the "fit" and in effect discouraging the unfit. Moreover, if these huge sums of philanthropic capital were to be justified, they had to exert a discernable influence, to make things happen that would not otherwise occur. Sears noted the position of the General Education Board, that institutions that could not find a constituency of supporters in their own community were not deserving of foundation gifts (p. 95). In application, this approach tended to hold up the standards of the stronger institutions as the canons of proper practice. Sears described this process, yet resisted the obvious conclusion. He denied that the foundations served as a standardizing agency (p. 98), when in fact their actions had just that effect.

The Carnegie Foundation for the Advancement of Teaching specifically intended its actions to serve as a "centralizing and standarding influence in American education," and the General Education Board similarly wished to eliminate "waste and confusion."[29] The latter sought to determine "scientifically" (p.94) the colleges it would aid by requiring adherence to the financial practices of the wealthy institutions. These included such measures as absolute fiscal separation of college from preparatory department and the maintenance of an inviolate endowment. The Carnegie Foundation had to be even more systematic in determining the limited number of institutions whose faculty would qualify for pensions. In this process, it induced numerous colleges to accept a common standard for high-school preparation (Carnegie units) and to dispense with denominational affiliation. In sponsoring the devastating Flexner Report, the foundation helped to impose the more rigorous model of medical education favored by the American Medical Association. Most of these measures were clearly to the benefit of American higher education, but they constituted a rather deliberate policy of standardization on the part of the foundations, and they helped to cause the considerable attrition of weaker institutions that occurred during these years.[30]

With greater historical perspective, and with the benefit of two subsequent generations of historical scholarship, it is possible to see more clearly the ways in which philanthropy affected the development of American higher education. Certainly some of these effects provide cause for misgiving. For the most part, however, the questionable developments that have been associated with philanthropy have in the long run turned out to have positive consequences as well. Alumni giving undoubtedly exacerbated the social exclusiveness of the Eastern-endowed colleges for some time, but the very affluence thereby produced strongly abetted their eventual transition to highly meritocratic admissions procedures. Foundation policy continued to favor the strong during the 1920s, when Wickliffe Rose, Director of the General Education Board, proclaimed his intentions to make the peaks of American higher education even higher; but the steep institutional hierarchy that his actions accentuated was instrumental in furthering the ascendency of American science, a development of undoubted beneficial effects.[31] By the same token, today philanthropy would seem, by virtue of exploiting the deep loyalties that sports engender, to be an accomplice to the excesses associated with big-time athletics.

In the main, and with these kinds of exceptions, it would still seem that the sanguine case that Sears made for educational philanthropy would basically hold. Unlike the situation created by the so-called "dead hand," American educational philanthropy did not preserve large amounts of capital for dubious social purposes. Rather, Sears's history shows how voluntary support was the mainstay of American colleges and universities before the twentieth century, and, as he rightly emphasizes, most of this support went to underwriting core educational activities. He might have added that private giving has greatly abetted the relative abundance of resources and the diverse institutional orientations that have allowed the American system of higher education to become the most extensive in the world. For that reason, philanthropy has constituted a crucial factor in the evolution of American colleges and universities and has been an important facet of the interaction of those institutions with American society. Jesse Sears's pioneering study provides an overview of this process and, as he himself would have proudly pointed out, an abundance of facts. He thereby provided an important beginning to the study of philanthropy in the history of American higher education. Perhaps the re-publication of this work and a wider circulation will help to attract to this relatively neglected subject scholarly attention commensurate with its importance.

Notes

1. Merle Curti and Roderick Nash, *Philanthropy in the Shaping of American Higher Education* (New Brunswick, New Jersey: Rutgers University Press, 1965), p. 316.
2. Jesse B. Sears, *Jesse Brundage Sears: An Autobiography* (Palo Alto, California, 1959), Stanford University Archives, p. 34. The biographical material that follows has been taken from this document.
3. Jesse B. Sears and Adin D. Henderson, *Cubberley of Stanford and His Contribution to American Education* (Stanford: Stanford University Press, 1957), pp. 51–103, 258–65.
4. Lawrence A. Cremin, David A. Shannon, and Mary Evelyn Townsend, *A History of Teachers College, Columbia University* (New York: Columbia University Press, 1954), p. 42.
5. Lawrence A. Cremin, *The Wonderful World of Ellwood Patterson Cubberley: An Essay on the Historiography of American Education* (New York: Teachers College, Columbia University, 1965); Bernard Bailyn, *Education in the Forming of American Society* (Chapel Hill: University of North Carolina Press, 1960), p. 10.
6. Sears and Henderson, *Cubberley of Stanford*, pp. 124–26.

7. Cremin, *Wonderful World*, p. 25.

8. Paul Monroe, *A Textbook in the History of Education* (New York: Macmillan, 1932), p. 722.

9. Cf. *A Cyclopedia of Education*, "Endowments, Educational," Vol. 2, pp. 452–59, which was written by a British scholar (Arthur F. Leach) with some assistance from another Monroe student (Isaac L. Kandel) and a section by the editor on endowments in American higher education.

10. *A Cyclopedia of Education*, Vol. 4, pp. 668–71.

11. Sears, *Autobiography*, pp. 49–52; personal communication to the author from Robert Sears, son of J. B. Sears, Palto Alto, California, 6 June, 1988.

12. Jesse B. Sears, *The School Survey: A Textbook on the Use of School Surveying in the Administration of Public Schools* (New York: Houghton Mifflin, 1925), p. vii.

13. Margery Somers Foster, *'Out of smalle beginnings...': An Economic History of Harvard College in the Puritan Period (1626 to 1712)* (Cambridge, Massachusetts: Harvard University Press, 1962).

14. Jurgen Herbst, *Crisis to Crisis: American College Government, 1636–1819* (Cambridge, Massachusetts: Harvard University Press, 1982).

15. Beverly McAnear, "The Raising of Funds by the Colonial Colleges," *Mississippi Valley Historical Review* 39 (1952):591–612.

16. Curti and Nash, *Philanthropy in the Shaping*, pp. 33–35.

17. David B. Potts, " 'College Enthusiasm!' As Public Response, 1800–1860," *Harvard Education Review* 47 (1977):28–42; Colin B. Burke, *American Collegiate Populations: A Test of the Traditional View* (New York: New York University Press, 1982), pp. 42–44.

18. Frederick Rudolph, *The American College and University: A History* (New York: Random House, 1962), pp. 193–200.

19. For the special case of Harvard, see Ronald Story, *The Forging of an Aristrocracy: Harvard and the Boston Upper Class, 1800–1870* (Middletown, Connecticut: Wesleyan University Press, 1980).

20. Roger L. Geiger, *To Advance Knowledge: The Growth of American Research Universities, 1900–1940* (New York: Oxford University Press, 1986).

21. *Giving USA: 1984 Annual Report*, p. 55. These two proportions are not comparable, because Sears tabulated only large gifts, and the figures reported in *Giving USA* estimate total giving. Religion, which must be seriously undercounted in Sears's methodology, accounts for nearly half of all giving currently; Education vies with health/hospitals for second place.

22. Laurence R. Veysey, *The Emergence of the American University* (Chicago: University of Chicago Press, 1965), pp. 165–71; 347–50; 400–7.

23. Edward Shils, "The American Private University," *Minerva* 11 (1973):6–29.

24. Geiger, *To Advance Knowledge*, pp. 52–53.

25. Ibid., pp. 47–57; Roger L. Geiger, "After the Emergence: Voluntary Support and the Building of American Research Universities," *History of Education Quarterly* 25 (1985):369–81.

26. In terms of total wealth, theoretically the sum of all physical and financial capital, Harvard has always been the most affluent American institution of higher education. The Harvard endowment, however, at least on paper, was exceeded early in the twentieth century by those of Columbia and Stanford. A more meaningful measure of financial strength would be annual income from endowment; on this basis Harvard emerged preeminent by 1919, and Yale claimed the second spot during the 1920s. These data are given in Geiger, *To Advance Knowledge*, 274–77.

27. *Ibid.*, pp. 54–55; 123–37.

28. Barry D. Karl and Stanley N. Katz, "The American Private Philanthropic Foundation and the Public Sphere, 1890–1930," *Minerva* 19 (1981):236–70.

29. *The General Education Board: An Account of Its Activities, 1902–1914* (New York: General Education Board, 1915), pp. 103–16; Henry S. Pritchett, "Mr. Carnegie's Gift to the Teachers," *The Outlook*, May 19, 1906, p. 125; see also Ellen Condliffe Lagemann, *Private Power for the Public Good* (Middletown, Connecticut: Wesleyan University Press, 1983), pp. 39–41.

30. The number of medical schools decreased from 155 in 1910 to 85 in 1920. More generally, the number of colleges and universities remained almost constant (c 1000) from 1890 to 1920, even though enrolments almost quadrupled. Because institutional foundings were frequent during these years, many colleges must have been closing. This phenomenon has not received the study it deserves.

31. Geiger, *To Advance Knowledge*, pp. 161–64 and passim.

INTRODUCTION.

This study represents an attempt to trace the influence of philanthropy in the development of higher education in America. Incident to this has been the further question of what has been evolved by way of a theory of educational endowments, or, broader still, of educational philanthropy. The importance of such a study is obvious when we consider the part philanthropy has played in the development of the American college and university. Its importance is equally clear, too, when we view the recent enormous increase in educatonal philanthropy, and the wide variety of educational enterprises to which philanthropy is giving rise. If we are to avoid the waste that must inevitably come from bad management of gifts, from wrong dispositions of money over which the future can exercise no control, we must study our already extensive experience and develop a set of guiding principles or a fundamental theory of educational philanthropy.

It was evident from the outset that any reasonably brief treatment of a subject occupying so large a place in the history of American higher education would present certain difficulties, not only in the selection of facts, but also in the interpretation of the comparatively small amount of first-hand data that could be satisfactorily treated in brief space.

It has been the writer's purpose carefully to scrutinize the materials presented to see that they were fully representative of one or another important type of philanthropy affecting our higher education; to see that no type of effort was without representation; to draw only such conclusions as the facts clearly warranted; and, finally, to present the data in such form as to make them fully available for future use in more intensive studies, if occasion for such should arise. If in these respects the effort has been successful, then it is believed to offer, in broad outline, the history of philanthropy in the development of American higher institutions of learning. As such it is presented, with the hope that it may add somewhat to the general perspective we now possess for the various features of our institutions for higher training, and to the development of a sound theory of educational philanthropy, as well as with a full consciousness that there is very much yet to be done before we shall have adeqauate details concerning any one of the many phases of this problem.

At the beginning of our experience in this field Europe had formulated no theory of educational endowment or of educational philanthropy, but subsequently the subject received treatment in the writings of their social and political philosophers, and also to no less extent by practical statesmen engaged in correcting the evils of past mistakes in practice. These ideas have been traced briefly in an introductory chapter. Following this, it has been my purpose to describe our own practice from the beginning to the present time, and to make such generalizations as the facts seemed to warrant. Two types of data have been studied: First, the foundation documents, such as charters, articles of incorporation, constitutions, by-laws, deeds of trust, wills, and conditions controlling gifts on the one hand; and, second, the statistics of gifts on the other. To add to the value of bare description, the comparative method has been utilized wherever it was possible.

The writer is indebted to numerous librarians and education boards for special courtesies, and especially to Dr. Paul Monroe, not only for having suggested this problem, but also for important suggestions concerning the method of its treatment.

The original study of which this bulletin is a condensation is on file at Teachers College, Columbia University, where it was presented in April, 1919, in partial fulfillment of the requirements for the degree of doctor of philosophy.

J. B. SEARS.

STANFORD UNIVERSITY, CALIF.,
  April 20, 1919.

PHILANTHROPY IN THE HISTORY OF AMERICAN HIGHER EDUCATION.

Chapter I.

DEVELOPMENT OF A THEORY OF PHILANTHROPY.

THE EARLY CONCEPTION OF PHILANTHROPY.

So long as charity remained intimately associated with the church it is not strange that the work it was doing should never have been called in question. The term "charity" meant Christian virtue, and its economic significance was wholly overlooked. In praising a man's good intentions it was not thought important that society should hold him responsible for having wisdom in expressing them.

PLACE OF EDUCATIONAL FOUNDATIONS IN TURGOT'S SOCIAL THEORY.

It is left, therefore, to the economist to look critically into the problem so long ignored by superstition, religion, and sentimentalism. It is interesting to note that it was in an age when all social life was being carefully scrutinized that Turgot published his unsigned article "Foundations," in the *Encyclopedia*, in 1757. It is at this point that a real halt is called, and philanthropy becomes a problem for the intellect.

All peoples and ages have regarded active benevolence as an important virtue, and to such acts the severest economist offers no protest. But the bald unwisdom evident in the presumption that man is competent to judge what is good for all the future is what drew from Turgot this classic criticism, which John Morley says is "the most masterly discussion we possess of the advantages and disadvantages of endowments."[1]

The native instinct which underlies man's desire to relieve his brother in distress makes no distinction between present and future good; nor does it discover that good is a relative term. Consequently, it is not strange that much evil is done where only good is intended. But add to this native impulse the best wisdom of our day and yet we can not say what will be the need of another generation; and if we could, and were large-hearted enough to endow that need, we would not be able to guarantee that our successors, in whose

---

[1] John Morley: Diderot and the Encyclopaedists, p. 191.

1

hands we place the right, would execute with the same enthusiasm with which we have founded. Business, but not enthusiasm, may be handed down.

It is because the history of European endowments was written so plainly in these terms across the faces of the church, the hospital, and the school, that Turgot was lead to inquire into the general utility of foundations, with a view to demonstrating their impropriety. He does not approach the subject in a purely abstract way, though he had a well-defined social theory which later received a clear statement in his "Reflexions sur la Formation et la Distribution des Richesses," since for every principle set forth he appeals to history for its justification.

Turgot sees so little good accomplished by endowments that he is led to say: "Un fondateur est un homme qui veut éterniser l'effet de ses volonté." [2] His motive may be good, but results prove his lack of wisdom. After citing cases which are convincing, he concludes: "Je ne craindrai point de dire que, si l'on comparait les advantages et les inconvénients de toutes les fondations qui existent aujourd'hui en Europe, il n'y en aurait peut-être pas une qui soutint l'examen d' une politique éclairé." [3] Granting that at its conception the object is a real utility, there is yet the impossibility of its future execution to be reckoned with, because the enthusiasm of the founder can not be transmitted. If even this, however, were overcome, it would still not be long till time would sweep away the utility, for society has not always the same needs.

Thus Turgot pointed out the difficulties and the consequent evils inherently connected with the establishment of perpetuities. If we suggest the idea of a periodical revision, which is done by later thinkers, Turgot quickly points to history and shows how long periods usually elapse after a foundation has become useless before its uselessness is detected; that those closely acquainted with such a charity are so accustomed to its working as not to be struck by its defects and that those not acquainted have little chance of observing its weakness. Then there is the difficulty of determining the proper character and extent of the modifications, to say nothing of enforcing its adoption against the opposition of the vested interests.

The author distinguishes two kinds of social needs which are intended to be fulfilled by foundations: One, "appartiennent à la sociéte entière, et ne seront que le résultant des intérêts de chacune de ses parties: tels sont les besoins généraux de l' humanité, la nourriture pour tous les hommes, les bonnes moeurs et l' éducation des enfants, pour toutes les familles; et cet intérêt est plus ou moins pressant pour les différents besoins; car un homme sent plus vivement le besoin de la nourriture que l' intérêt qu'il a de donner à ses enfants une bonne éducation." [4] This need, he says, can not be fulfilled by a foundation or any sort of gratuitous means, for the general good must result from the efforts of each individual in behalf of his own interests. It is the business of the state to destroy obstacles which impede man in his industry or in the enjoyment of its fruits. Similarly, he insists that every family owes to its children an education, and that only through these individual efforts can the general perfection of education arise. If interest in education is lacking, he would arouse it by means of a system of prizes given on merit.

The second class of public needs he would propose to meet by foundations he has classed as accidental, limited in place and time, having less to do with a general system of administration, and that may demand particular relief, such, for instance, as the support of some old men, the hardship of a scarcity, or an

---

[2] Turgot-Oeuvres, Vol. I, p. 300.
[3] Ibid., p. 301.
[4] Ibid., p. 305.

epidemic, etc. For the amelioration of such needs he would employ the public revenues of the community, some contribution of all its members, and voluntary subscriptions from generous citizens. This scheme he declares to be not only efficient but impossible of abuse, for the moment funds are diverted from their proper use their source will at once dry up. This puts no money into luxury or useless buildings, it would withdraw no funds from general circulation, and place no land in idle hands. He points to the success of such associations in England, Scotland, and Ireland, and thus supports his theory with reference to present practice.

By these lines of thought he justifies the proposition that government has a right to dispose of old foundations. " L'utilité publique est la loi suprêm," [5] he says, and adds that a superstitious regard for the intention of the founder ought not to nullify it.

These are the principles, not deduced from an imaginary law of nature alone, but carefully supported and justified at each point by the clear facts of history. All foundations are condemned by Turgot as worse than useless and his laissez faire doctrine would forbid the establishment of others. This was a bold doctrine to preach in the middle of the eighteenth century, but its impress was felt throughout Europe, and it is only a few decades till another member of the same school of economists lends support to these views.

PLACE OF EDUCATIONAL FOUNDATIONS IN ADAM SMITH'S FREE-TRADE ECONOMY.

Adam Smith's " Wealth of Nations," first published in 1776, tends to substantiate all Turgot had taught and to show that it applies particularly to educational endowments. In discussing the natural inequalities of labor and stock, he insists that where there is " perfect liberty " all advantages and disadvantages tend to equality.[6] And in the following chapter on political inequalities of wages and profit he points out three ways in which political interference with " perfect liberty " has produced great and important inequalities. " First, by restraining the competition in some employments to a smaller number than would otherwise be disposed to enter into them ; secondly, by increasing it in others beyond what it naturally would be ; and thirdly, by obstructing the free circulation of labor and stock, both from employment to employment and from place to place." [7]

In support of the second he shows how public money, " and sometimes the piety of private founders," [8] have drawn many people into the profession of the clergy, thereby increasing competition to the point of making the salaries very low. Exactly the same thing, he says, has happened to men of letters and to teachers, and when contrasted with the time of Isocrates, " before any charities of this kind had been established for the education of indigent people to the learned professions," [9] the ill effect upon the teacher's income is evident enough.

There is yet another phase of the subject which is touched upon in Smith's discussion of the expense of the institutions for the education of the youth. Referring to the many endowed schools throughout Europe, he asks:

Have those public endowments contributed in general to promote the end of their institution? Have they contributed to encourage the diligence and to improve the abilities of the teachers? Have they directed the course of education toward objects more useful, both to the individual and to the public, than those to which it would naturally have gone of its own accord? [10]

[5] Turgot-Oeuvres, Vol. I, p. 308.
[6] Smith, Adam : Wealth of Nations, Bk. I, Ch. X, p. 101.
[7] Ibid., p. 121.
[8] Ibid., p. 131.
[9] Ibid., p. 134.
[10] Ibid., p. 249.

He then states as a universal principle that the exertion of most people in a profession is proportional to the necessity they are under of making that exertion. He believes that the endowments of schools have diminished the necessity of application in the teachers, and shows how the older and richer colleges have clung longest to a useless and worn-out curriculum, while the poorer universities, dependent upon their popularity for much of their income, introduced the modern subjects much earlier.[11] He says:

Were there no public institutions for education, no systems, no sciences would be taught for which there was not some demand, or which the circumstances of the times did not render it either necessary or convenient, or at least fashionable, to learn.[12]

This extreme application of the principle of free trade is modified only slightly by Smith to meet the inequality of opportunity brought about in a complex society where division of labor has been carried to great length. While he states that in most cases the state of society places the greater number of individuals in such situations as form in them almost all the abilities and virtues which that state requires, yet there are cases in which this is not true.

The man whose whole life is spent in performing a few simple operations, of which the effects, too, are perhaps always the same, or very nearly the same, has no occasion to exert his understanding or to exercise his invention in finding out expedients for removing difficulties which never occur. He naturally loses, therefore, the habit of such exertion, and generally becomes as stupid and ignorant as it is possible for a human creature to become.[13]

Thus Smith would have the state intervene in behalf of the great labor population, whose intellectual tendency must inevitably be in this direction.

This brief presentation of Smith's attitude toward perpetuities shows how his principles of social organization exclude them; and, like Turgot's, his theory is constructed in the presence of existing facts. The sum of the contribution is little more than a specific application of Turgot's arguments to educational foundations.

If the social theory underlying the objections to endowments made by these two men is sound, surely the facts they have cited would warrant their conclusion that endowments are evil because they interfere with the real laws of human progress. Certainly the evidence they cite makes clear the difficulties attending their establishment.

Is a laissez faire policy a sound basis for social organization, and can these evil practices be overcome? These are problems for their successors.

WILLIAM VON HUMBOLDT'S THEORY.

William von Humboldt wrote, in 1791: " Ueberhaupt soll die Erziehung nur, ohne Rüksicht auf bestimmte, den Menschen zu ertheilende bürgerliche Formen, Menschen bilden; so bedarf es des Staats nicht."[14] Thus he not only accepts the system of free exchange laid down by Turgot and Smith, but excludes the possible modification which Turgot implies under the head of "accidental" social needs, and which Smith makes to correct the slight disadvantage to which some are placed by the effects of the extreme division of labor. "Unter freren Menschen gewunen alle Gewerbe bessren Fortgang; blühen alle Künste schöner auf; erweitern sich alle Wissenschaften," says William von Humboldt,

---

[11] This argument is quite obviously beside the mark in America.
[12] Smith, Adam: Wealth of Nations, Bk. V, Ch. I, p. 266.
[13] Ibid., p. 267.
[14] Wilhelm von Humboldt, Werke, Vol. VII, p. 57.

and again, "Bei freuen Menschen entsteht Nacheiferung, und es bilden sich bessere Erzieher wo ihr Schiksal von dem Erfolg ihrer Arbeiten, als wo es von der Beförderung abhängt, die sie vom Staate zu erwarten haben."

Here we find a leading German statesman insisting upon these social and economic principles in matters of education. Surely he did not foresee the future development of schools in Germany, where the State has been responsible for practically all educational work.

While our purpose here is not to write, or even to sketch, the history of economic theory, yet it is interesting to note that the objections soon to be raised against a wholesale condemnation of educational endowments are focused upon the economic doctrine of the physiocrats, and fit in as early steps in the historical decline of the laissez faire economy.

CHALMERS'S MODIFICATION OF THE EARLIER THEORIES.

Dr. Thomas Chalmers, an early nineteenth century economist, interested in the practical problem of handling the poor, accepts the idea of free exchange to the extent of condemning the state endowment of pauperism but urges that an endowment for the relief of indigence is not to be compared with one whose object is the support of literary or Christian instruction. For education, though it is a real want, is not a felt want. ' He says:

The two cases, so far from being at all alike in principles, stand in direct and diametric opposition to each other. We desiderate the latter endowment because of the languor of the intellectual or sp.ritual appetency; in so much that men, left to themselves, seldom or never originate a movement toward learning. We deprecate the former endowment because, in the strength of the physical appetency, we have the surest guarantee that men will do their uttermost for good; and a public charity having this for its object by lessening the industry and forethought that would have been otherwise put forth in the cause, both adds to the wants and detracts from the real work and virtue of the species. And, besides, there is no such strength of compassion for the sufferings of the moral or spiritual that there is for the physical destitution. An endowment for education may be necessary to supplement the one, while an endowment for charity may do the greatest moral and economic mischief by superseding the other. Relatives and neighbors could bear to see a man ignorant or even vicious. They could not bear to see him starve.[15]

Thus an important modification of the above social theory is proposed. Whether the practical philanthropist has since shown such discrimination or not, the principle involved in the criticism was important. Shall the provision for education be dependent upon the mere demand of the market, or shall this important but " unfelt " need be stimulated by some kind of endowment?

MILL'S OPPOSITION TO THE THEORIES OF TURGOT AND SMITH.

In February, 1833, John Stuart Mill published an article in the Jurist [16] in which he declared ignorance and want of culture to be the sources of all social evil, and adds that they can not be met by political checks.[17] He says:

There is also an unfortunate peculiarity attending these evils. Of all calamities, they are those of which the persons suffering from them are apt to be least aware. Of their bodily wants and ailments, mankind are generally conscious; but the wants of the mind, the want of being wiser and better, is, in the far greater number of cases, unfelt; some of its disastrous consequences are felt, but are ascribed to any imaginable cause except the true one.[18]

15 Quoted by Thos. Mackay in " The State and Charity," p. 36.
16 Later published in " Dissertations and Discussions," Vol. I, pp. 28–68.
17 Mill, J. S. : " Dissertations and Discussions," Vol. I, p. 54.
18 Ibid., pp. 54, 55.

In answer to the question as to what men have depended upon and must depend upon for the removal of their ignorance and defects of culture, he says, "mainly on the unremitting exertions of the more instructed and cultivated," which, he adds, is a wide field of usefulness open for foundations. He combats Smith's argument that such foundations are but premiums on idleness and insufficiency merely by saying that such is the case only when it is nobody's business to see that the trust is duly executed.

To show further how the idea of endowments fits into Mill's general social philosophy, note what he says in his essay "On Liberty," written in 1858:

With regard to the merely contingent, or, as it may be called, constructive injury which a person causes to society, by conduct which neither violates any specific duty to the public, nor occasions perceptible hurt to any assignable individual except himself, the inconvenience is one which society can afford to bear, for the sake of the greater good of human freedom.[19]

Individual freedom is as carefully guarded as by Turgot or Smith, but the implication that it is best preserved by a complete system of free exchange is carefully avoided.

Mill does not believe that in a government where majority rule predominates the ideas of the minority should be lost. In his essay on "Endowments," published in the Fortnightly Review, April 1, 1869, he says:

There is good reason against allowing them to do this (make bequests) in favor of an unborn individual whom they can not know, or a public purpose beyond the probable limits of human foresight. But within those limits, the more scope that is given to varieties of human individuality the better.

And,

Since trial alone can decide whether any particular experiment is successful, latitude should be given for carrying on the experiment until the trial is complete.[20]

His contention is, then, not only that foundations should be permitted, but that over a reasonable period of time the exact wishes of the founder should be strictly adhered to. His defense, later in the essay, of a foundation just then being severely criticized by the press shows the great social import which he attaches to the preservation of an unusual idea of an unusual person. After a complete trial of the experiment has been effected, the obligation of society to the founder has been discharged, and the value of the gift to society can be indicated.

The explanation of this relationship is the first object of the essay of 1833, the second being a discussion of the spirit in which and the reservations with which the legislature should proceed to accept and modify the original plan and object of the foundation. In brief, he regards the endowment as public property after about fifty years from the date of its establishment, and in every sense subject to the will of society, even to changing the purpose of the gift, if necessary, to meet the changes of succeeding ages.

Mill's economic justification of man's right to establish endowments is quite as interesting as his social justification. He says that it is due not to the children but to the parents that they should have the power of bestowing their wealth according to their own preference and judgment, for—

Bequest is one of the attributes of property; the ownership of a thing can not be looked upon as complete without the power of bestowing it, at death or

---

[19] Mill, J. S.: "On Liberty," published in the Harvard Classics, p. 289.

[20] Mill, J. S.: "Endowments," Fort. Rev., vol. 5, p. 380. See also essay on "The Right and Wrong of State Interference with Corporate and Church Property," in "Dissertations and Discussions," p. 32.

during life, at the owner's pleasure; and all the reasons which recommend that private property should exist recommend pro tanto extension of it.[21]

This is no small modification of the theories of Turgot and Smith, and is a definite stand taken by Mill in respect not only to a philosophical but to an important practical issue then before the English public. And only a few years before his death he wrote in his autobiography[22] that the position he had taken in 1833 was as clear as he could now make it. Indeed, this very principle of Mill's was in 1853 embodied in the legislative enactment carried through by Lord Brougham and others.

MR. LOWE'S RETURN TO FREE TRADE PRINCIPLES.

Mill's position, however, was too conservative, and too considerate of the numerous abuses of endowments then so well known to everyone, and drew forth sharp criticisms.[23] In condemning the report of the commissioners appointed to inquire into middle-class education, whose procedure had been generally in line with the ideas of Mill and Chalmers, Mr. Lowe[24] (later Lord Sherbrooke) calls for a return to the ordinary rules of political economy. He would class teaching as a trade, and keep it in the quickening atmosphere of free exchange. This return to the notion that failure of endowments is due not to founder worship, as Mill would say, but to the principle of endowment, shows the influence of the free-trade economy.

In practice at this time the cry is not that all foundations be used to pay the national debt, and so place education where Mr. Lowe would ask, but rather how can the terrible waste of funds be checked, or, what system of control can the State legitimately exercise? We have Mill's suggestion that society will progress most rapidly when it gives wide range to social and educational experimentation, and that this is done best, not by the State through a commission, which would tend to force all endowments into a uniform mold, but by legal enforcement of the exact conditions of the foundation till the merits of the experiment become evident.

HOBHOUSE ON " THE DEAD HAND " IN EDUCATION.

During the period 1868 to 1879 Sir Arthur Hobhouse delivered a series of addresses, afterwards published as " The Dead Hand," [25] in which he accepts, with Mill, both the principle of endowed education and the idea that every such bequest should be made to serve the present. The question of method, however, is a point on which he takes issue with Mill. He can not see that the term " property " implies power of posthumous disposition. Tried by history, he says, " the further back we trace any system of laws, the smaller we find the power of posthumous disposition to be." [26] Furthermore, he insists that 250 years of English experience does not reveal one useful educational experiment resulting from such foundations as Mr. Mill regards important in the development of new ideas and lines of social and educational practice.[27]

[21] Mill, J. S. : " Political Economy," Vol. I, p. 287.
[22] Autobiography, p. 182.
[23] See Report of Schools Inquiry Commission of 1868.
[24] See his Middle Class Education, Endowment or " Free Trade."
[25] London, 1880.
[26] Hobhouse, Sir A. : " The Dead Hand," p. 14.
[27] Ibid., p. 94.

This attitude is further emphasized by Sir Joshua Fitch, whose practical contact with English educational endowments gives weight to his words when he says:

One uniform purpose is manifest in the testaments, the deeds of gift and the early statutes by which the character of these schools was intended to be shaped. It is to encourage the pursuit of a liberal education founded on the ancient languages.[28]

Further, in his analysis of the motives which have prompted bequests to public uses, Hobhouse does not find justification for Mill's position. In the list of motives which he finds underlying the foundations in England are: Love of power and certain cognate passions, ostentatiousness, vanity, superstition, patriotism to a slight extent, and spite.[29] While this list might not fit individual cases, he insists that it is true for the mass.

Mill thinks that the public does not know its own needs fully, because it is only the majority speaking. Hobhouse regards the public as an individual competent to judge its needs and naturally endowed with the right to express them; hence he would lay down two principles upon which all foundations must be established: First, "If the public is chosen as legatee, the legacy shall be, as it ought to be, an unconditional one";[30] and, second, "there shall always be a living and reasonable owner of property, to manage it according to the wants of mankind."[31] The excuse for such a title to his book here becomes evident. He can not see that the living have need for the continual advice and control of the dead.

OTHER ENGLISH THEORIES.

As interest in education grew in England, respect for perpetual trusts decreased. The act of 1853 above referred to, giving a commission power only to inquire into and report the condition of charitable foundations, was later revised giving the commission greater power. And finally, in 1869, one year after the report of the School Inquiry Commission, we have the "Endowed schools act,"[32] giving the commissioners power to "render any educational endowment most conducive to the advancement of the education of boys and girls,"[33] etc. This act was somewhat strengthened by revision in 1873 and again in 1874.[34]

During the last half of the nineteenth century there was wide discussion of the practical problem in England, but little of theoretical value was added. Sir Joshua Fitch, in an address at Pennsylvania University,[35] lays down two principles: First, an endowment's only right to exist is its benefit to the community; and, second, the State is the supreme trustee of all endowments. Thomas Hare, in 1869,[36] regards all property as either public or private. An endowment, being public property, is subject to the public will. Before the Social Science Association,[37] he accepts Mill's notion of endowments as valuable social and educational experiments, and insists only upon the State's right of supervision.

SUMMARY AND CONCLUSION.

Many other writers have added bits of practical wisdom, but the results of more than a hundred years of theorizing may be briefly summed up as follows:

[28] Fitch, Joshua: "Educational Aims and Methods," p. 191.
[29] Hobhouse, Sir A.: "The Dead Hand," p. 15 ff.
[30] Fitch, Joshua: "Educational Aims and Methods," p. 120.
[31] Ibid., p. 121.
[32] See 32 and 33 Vict., C. 56.
[33] Title: "The Endowed Schools Act, 1869" (32 and 33 Vict., C. 56).
[34] 36 and 37 Vict., C. 87, and 37 and 38 Vict., C. 87.
[35] Published in "Educational Aims and Methods."
[36] Fortnightly Rev., 5, 284–297.
[37] Trans. Soc. Sc. Assoc., 1869, p. 132.

There is perhaps no universally acceptable theory of educational endowments yet worked out; the early free-trade economy has been tempered by substantially removing education from its scope; the experimental value of the endowed school is accepted on the ground that social progress is dependent quite as much upon the ideas and interests of the minority as upon those of the majority, and that with wide variation in educational endeavor, opportunity for wise selection is increased; that endowments are public property, since they are given to public service, and should therefore be subject to such public supervision as will prevent their being wasted or becoming socially obnoxious.

Recalling Turgot's position, we can see that his statement of the meaning and function of foundations is yet a fairly acceptable presentation of the philosophical problem.

Chapter II.
THE COLONIAL PERIOD.

INFLUENCES AFFECTING THE BEGINNING OF AMERICAN HIGHER
EDUCATION.

1. THE PROBLEM.

In early colonial America there was little theorizing as to who should build colleges or as to how such schools should be financed. From the beginning higher education was a serious interest of the people, and one which early found practical expression. What the scholars and statesmen thought of endowments, therefore, we can infer only from what they actually did. They faced college building as a practical problem, and whatever we have since developed by way of a theory of endowed education in America we have developed very largely out of our long and varied experience.

In this and succeeding chapters, therefore, it is the purpose to assemble facts which will adequately describe that experience, to the end that the character and extent of the influence which philanthropy has had in the development of higher education in America may be seen. Finally, from an interpretation of these facts it should then be possible to state whatever theory of endowments there has been evolved in this country.

When in the early history of Harvard College we find among its donors the general court, numerous towns and churches, as well as individuals, we realize that it is necessary to define the term "philanthropy." In this study the term is used to include all gifts except those from State. Again, if, as we are told, philanthropy means an expression of love for mankind, the names of Eleazer Wheelock, Theodorus J. Frelinghuysen, Morgan Edward, James Blair, and other notable ministers of the gospel would loom large in the description. However important the work of such men may have been, it would be impossible satisfactorily to show its results in a study which is designed to be quite largely quantitative. Accordingly, this study will be concerned with only those facts and forces which play some measurable part in shaping our institutions of higher learning.

2. COLLEGE CHARTERS ANALYZED.

The forces which entered into the founding of our first colleges were many and complex. Certain of these stood out clearly and for many years played a large part in directing the growth of higher learning. Everywhere and particularly in the foundation documents of the colonial colleges we are able to see these forces at work, giving form to these infant institutions. In Table 1 are shown such data, taken from the charters of the nine colonial colleges.

10

English influences are suggested by the three names, William and Mary, King's, and Queen's. To these Dartmouth must be added, having taken its name in honor of its chief benefactor, Lord Dartmouth, of England, and, for a similar reason, Yale. Further, important subscriptions were collected in England: £10,000 for Dartmouth; $4,500 for Brown; £2,500 for William and Mary in addition to the gift of the English Government of £2,000 and 20,000 acres of land; King's and Pennsylvania together, some £10,000;[1] and over £2,000 for Princeton.[2] In all cases these subscriptions furnished relatively large sums for the colleges, and were among the early, and in case of William and Mary, Dartmouth and Brown, the founding gifts.

AIM OF THE COLLEGES—GIFTS EXPECTED.

Harvard University.—" Through the good hand of God " men " are moved and stirred up to give * * * for the advancement of all good literature, arts, and sciences." [3]

" Many well-devoted persons have been and daily are moved and stirred up to give and bestow sundry gifts, legacies, lands, and revenues for the advancement of all good literature, arts, and sciences in Harvard College."

College of William and Mary.—" That the Church of Virginia may be furnished with a seminary of ministers of the Gospel, and that the youth may be piously educated in good letters and manners and that the Christian faith may be propagated amongst the western Indians, to the glory of Almighty God ; to make a place of universal study, or perpetual college of divinity, philosophy, languages, and other good arts and sciences.

Yale University.—To found a school " Wherein Youth may be instructed in the Arts and Sciences, who through the blessings of Almighty God may be fitted for Public employment both in Church and Civil State."

" Several * * * men have expressed by Petition their earnest desires that full Liberty and Privilege be granted unto certain Undertakers for the founding, suitably endowing and ordering a Collegiate School," etc., also note further the power given to the trustees of the college.

Princeton University.—" For the instruction of youth in the learned languages and in the liberal arts and sciences." All religious sects to have equal educational opportunity.[4]

Columbia University.—" For Instruction and Education of Youth in the Learned Languages and in the Liberal Arts and Sciences." * * * "to lead them from the Study of Nature, to the Knowledge of themselves, and of the God of Nature, and their Duty to Him."

University of Pennsylvania.—The academy out of which the College grew was " for instructing youth for reward, as poor children on charity " " we, being desirous to encourage such pious, useful, and charitable designs." College is for instruction " in any kind of literature, arts, and sciences."

---

[1] Pennsylvania University Bulletin, Vol. III, p. 4, January, 1899, contains a copy of the " Fiat " for the Royal Brief, issued by King George III, granting the right to the two " Seminaries " to take the subscription.

[2] See Maclean: History of the College of New Jersey, Vol. I, 147 ff., for a discussion of this undertaking; also copies of some documents connected with it. The full amount of the subscription is not known.

[3] Charter was not granted till 1650. " New England's First Fruits " shows clearly the religious aim. Also the legislative act of 1642 uses the words *piety, morality,* and *learning* as expressing the aim of the college.

[4] See Princeton Univ. Catalogue, 1912–13, p. 46. The quotation is not from the charter, the first charter not being extant, but is from an advertisement in the Pennsylvania Gazette of Aug. 13, 1746–47. Nearly the same words are used in the charter of 1850 to express the aim of the college.

TABLE 1.—Data from the charters of the nine colonial colleges.

Date of founding.	History of name.	Why so named.	Movement for school started by whom.	First funds of college.			Control.	Charter.			
				Source.	Amount.	Form.		Requested by whom.	Granted by whom.	When granted.	First president's religious affiliation.
1635	"A school or college"; Harvard College, 1638.	Gift from John Harvard.	General Court of Massachusetts Bay.	General Court; John Harvard.	£400: £400 and library.	Grant; bequest.	General Court of Massachusetts Bay till 1642.	President Dunster.	General Court of Massachusetts Bay, with consent of governor.	1650	Educated at Magdalen College, Cambridge, England.
1692	College of William and Mary.	For the King and Queen of England.	Jas. Blair and 4 other of chief clergy of Virginia.	Blair's subscriptions in England; English Government.	£2,500; £2,000 and 20,000 acres.	Subscription; grant.	Self-perpetuating board of trustees, 18 in number, not exceeding 20.	Jas. Blair, agent for Virginia Assembly.	William and Mary of England.	1692	Clergyman of Church of England.
1701	The Collegiate School of Connecticut; Yale College, 1718.	Suggested in petition for charter; gift from Gov. Elihu Yale.	Ministers in New Haven Colony.	General Court of Connecticut.	£120; in country pay.	Grant....	Ten trustees, all ministers.[1]	Congregational clergy.	General Court of Connecticut.	1701	Congregational.
1746	College of New Jersey; Princeton University, 1896.	Located here on condition of a gift of 210 acres of land and a £1,000 Proc. money.[2]	Presbyterian clergy and laymen.				Board of trustees, 23 in number.	Presbyterian clergy.[3]	George II, through Governor of New Jersey, with his Council's consent.	1746; 1748	Presbyterian; Yale graduate in 1706.
1754	King's College; Columbia College, 1787.		Probably by Trinity Church.[4]	New York Legislature, by lottery.	£3,443.[5]......	Grant....	Board of 41 trustees (two-thirds of whom were of the Church of England.	Legislature......	Governor and Council of New York.	1754	Church of England, Yale graduate.
1755	College of Philadelphia; University of Pennsylvania, 1791.		Benj. Franklin..	The trustees and other charitable persons.		Subscription.	Board of trustees.	B. Franklin and other citizens.	Governor of Pennsylvania for the proprietors, T. and R. Penn.	1755	Church of England, Yale graduate.
1764	Rhode Island College; Brown University, 1804.	Brown University in honor of gift from Nicholas Brown.	Morgan Edwards and the Baptist Association of Philadelphia.	Collected in England and Ireland by Morgan Edwards.	$4,500......	Subscription.	Trustees, 36 in number, 22 of whom must be Baptists.	Philadelphia Baptist Association.	Governor of Rhode Island.	1765	Baptist Church.

1766	Queen's College; Rutgers College, 1825.	In honor of the royal consort, Charlotte; Col. Henry Rutger's support and leadership.	Theo. J. Frelinghuysen.	....	....	Board of trustees, 37 in number.	Progressive clergy and congregations of Dutch Reformed Church.	Governor of New Jersey in name of George III.	1766	Dutch Reformed Church.[6]
1769	Dartmouth College.	For its chief benefactor, Lord Dartmouth, of England.	Rev. Eleazer Wheelock, who opened school for Christianizing Indian youth in 1754.	Subscription in England.	£10,000.....	Subscription.	Twelve trustees.	Wheelock, who had kept the Indian school	Governor of the Province of New Hampshire.	1769

1 "Inhabiting within this colony, or the major part of them"; the board added one to its number, making 11.
2 College catalogue, 1912-13, p. 58.
3 Maclean: "History of the College of New Jersey," vol. 1, ch. 1, gives a complete account of the founding.
4 Moore, N. H.: "An Historical Sketch of Columbia College," p. 6.
5 This amount resulted from two lotteries authorized by legislative enactment, in 1746 and 1751. See "Hist. of Col. Univ., 1754-1904," p. 3 ff.
6 Murray: "Hist. of Educ. in N. J."; there was no president till 1783.

14 PHILANTHROPY IN AMERICAN HIGHER EDUCATION.

" Several benevolent and charitable persons have generously paid, and by subscriptions promised hereafter to pay, * * * for the use of said academy, divers sums of money," spent " in maintaining an academy there as well for the instruction of poor children on charity," etc." [5]

Brown University.—" And whereas a Public School or Seminary, * * * to which the Youth may freely resort for Education in the vernacular and learned Languages, and in the liberal Arts and Sciences would be for the general Advantage and Honor of the Government."

" And whereas Daniel Jenckes, Esq.; * * * with many others appear as undertakers in the valuable Design * * * praying that full Liberty and Power may be granted unto such of them, * * * to found, endow, * * * a College," etc. And, further, " Being willing to encourage * * * such an honorable and useful Institution, We, the said Governor," etc. [6]

Rutgers College.—The college is for " the Education of youth in the learned languages, liberal and useful arts and sciences, and especially in divinity." Did it try to preserve the Dutch language? [7]

Dartmouth College.—" Dartmouth College, for the education and instruction of Youth _ the Indian Tribes in * * * Learning * * * necessary * * * for civilizing and christianizing * * * Pagans * * * in Arts and Sciences; * * * also of English Youth."

" It hath been represented * * * that the Reverend Eleazer Wheelock * * * did * * *, at his own expense, * * * set on foot an Indian Charity school and for several years through the assistance of well-disposed Persons * * *," etc. [8]

3. RELIGIOUS AND DENOMINATIONAL INFLUENCES.

The religious influence is, of course, prominent. The statements showing how the movements for establishing the schools were started, those showing the source of control, the petitioners for the charters, and the religious affiliations of the first presidents, as well as the last one, showing the aim of the college, all point to religion as the large motivating force in the case of every one.

The beginning of William and Mary, Yale, Princeton, King's, Brown, Queen's, and Dartmouth (Harvard should probably be included) lies with groups of ministers or religious bodies. In the case of Yale, Princeton, Brown, Queen's, and Dartmouth the formal request for a charter was presented by representatives of religious bodies; while the source of control in the case of Yale, King's, and Brown was placed in the hands of religious bodies. In effect the same was true of Princeton, Harvard, and Queen's. All the first presidents were ministers.

It is in the charter, however, that the religious motive stands out with greatest prominence. The quotations presented are those which seem best to reveal the chief aim of the institution. Somewhere in every charter, Pennsylvania a possible exception, there is evidence that the teaching of religion was to be a prominent feature of the work of the college.

---

[5] Academy charter, in catalogue, 1912–13, p. 15. This is of course the basis of the charter for a college granted two years later.

[6] Charter, in catalogue in catalogue for 1912–13, pp. 29–30.

[7] Murray : " Hist. of Educ. in N. J.," p. 288, refers to the charter of 1770 as amending a statement which was said to have been included in the first charter, viz, that the Dutch language was to be used exclusively in the college.

[8] Charter, in Chase's Hist. of Dartmouth College and Hanover, N. H., p. 642.

To what extent denominationalism was a factor does not appear fully from this table. From other sources we know that the chancellorship of William and Mary was by charter granted to the Bishop of London; that Yale, which was built by Congregationalists in a Congregational colony, said in her charter that at least the major part of their 10 self-perpetuating trustees must always "be ministers of the Gospel inhabiting within this colony." [9] Princeton's charter does not call for denominational control, yet, according to the charter of 1648, there were 12 Presbyterian ministers on the board.[10] It is also true that Governor Morris, of New Jersey, refused Princeton's first request for a charter made, in his opinion, by a body of dissenters.[11]

These, as well as the connection which the schism in the Presbyterian Church in 1741–1745 had with the beginning of Princeton,[12] are evidence enough that denominationalism, if not even sectarianism, was a factor in its early life. In King's College about two-thirds of the 41 trustees were members of the Church of England, though they were not chosen officially upon religious grounds. The Pennsylvania College is an exception, for its charter shows its aim to have been broadly human, though not specifically religious, and certainly not denominational. By Brown's charter, however, 22 of her 36 trustees must be Baptists. There are no statements in the charters of Queen's and Dartmouth that they are to be controlled by certain religious sects, yet there is no doubt that the Dutch Reformed Church controlled Queen's and that Dartmouth was nonsectarian, but with half the board of trustees constituted of ministers,[13] the whole enterprise being threatened when the Reverend Wheelock refused to accept Governor Wentworth's proposal to make the Bishop of London an ex officio member of the board of trustees.[14] It is noticeable, too, that the formal request for the charter of Yale was made by a group of Congregational clergy, that of Princeton by Presbyterian clergy, that of Brown by the Philadelphia Baptist Association, and that of Queen's by the clergy and congregations of the Dutch Reformed Church.

The first president of Harvard was of Puritan training, and later was forced to resign because he agreed with the Anabaptists on the subject of infant baptism.[15] The first president of King's was a minister of the Church of England, and the inclusion of this requirement in the charter caused bitter opposition to the granting of the charter, a bitterness healed only by the addition of a professor of divinity "To be chosen by the Consistory of the (Dutch) Church for the time being." [16] The first rector (president) of Yale was a Congregational minister. Brown's first president was a Baptist minister, and Queen's a minister of the Dutch Church.

POLITICAL INFLUENCE.

The political influence is evident enough. Harvard was established by the colonial government. William and Mary was founded by the English and Virginia Governments, and Kings by the New York Legislature. Yale's charter

[9] Charter of the Collegiate School (Yale College) Catalogue, 1912–13, p. 64.
[10] Maclean : " History of the College of New Jersey," Vol. I, 92.
[11] Ibid., p. 34.
[12] Ibid., p. 24.
[13] Charter, in Chase, F., " History of Dartmouth College and Hanover, N. H., Vol. I, 642.
[14] Letter of Wheelock to Gov. Wentworth, of New Hampshire. See History of Dartmouth College and Hanover, N. H., by F. Chase, p. 115 ff.
[15] Pierce, Benjamin : " Hist. of Harvard Univ. from its Foundation, in the year 1636, to the Period of the Amer. Rev.," p. 10.
[16] Fulton, John. " Memoirs of Frederick A. P. Barnard," p. 302 ff. See also Ecclesiastical records of the State of New York.

says the youth are to be instructed to the end that "they may be fitted for public employment both in the church and civil state," and her first money gift was £120 country pay from the colony.

That these colleges were intended from the beginning to rest upon gifts of the people is suggested in the quotations from the charters given above. If not so stated, then the fact that the charter is granted to a body of men seeking to establish a college, together with the absence of any evidence that the state was accepting the responsibility, makes the inference clear. It is to be noted, too, that Harvard, Yale, Brown, Rutgers, and Dartmouth received their names from their first great benefactors, and that in only three cases were the first funds of the college granted by the legislatures.

To seek further evidence that the colonial colleges were or were not State institutions is not our present purpose. There is evidence here to show that the principle of State aid to higher education is as old as Harvard College. Yet the movement for each of the colleges, possibly excepting Harvard, was initiated either by a single man with great missionary zeal, or by a group of men, and not by the State.

From this preliminary examination of these foundation documents, then, one gathers some notion of the setting which our problem is to have. Judged by the facts presented, as well as in terms of the hard work associated with the starting of these institutions, philanthropy is clearly the mother of the colonial colleges.

FINANCES OF THE EARLY COLLEGES.

1. SCARCITY OF MONEY.

Down to 1693 we had but one college, that founded at Cambridge in 1635. There is probably nowhere available to-day a complete record of all the early gifts to Harvard, but what have been brought together here will doubtless give a fairly satisfactory exhibit of the nature and extent of the earliest philanthropy devoted to higher education in this country.

There is one thing so characteristic of the early gifts to all the colonial colleges that it must receive brief notice at the outset. That is, the size and kind of gifts. Harvard records the receipt "of a number of sheep bequeathed by one man, of a quantity of cotton cloth, worth 9 shillings, presented by another, of a pewter flagon, worth 10 shillings, by a third, of a fruit dish, a sugar spoon, a silver-tipt jug, one great salt, and one small trecher salt, by others." [17]   From Yale's early history the sentiment attaching to the words: "I give these books for founding a college in Connecticut," pronounced by each of the trustees as he placed his little contribution upon the table, could not be spared, and before a charter had been granted a formal gift of the "glass and nails which should be necessary to erect a college and hall" had been made,[18] Eleazar Wheelock, the founder and first president of Dartmouth, in a letter replying to criticisms of the "plainness of the surroundings" at the college, says: "As to the college, it owns but one (tablecloth), that was lately given by a generous lady in Connecticut, and of her own manufacture," [19] and again in a letter to the Honorable Commissioners for Indian Affairs, etc., he says, after indicating the impossible financial condition in which the college finds itself: "I have, with the assistance of a number of those who have contributed their old put-off clothing, supported them (the scholars) along hitherto." [20]   Doubtless similar examples could be

---

[17] Peirce: Hist. of Harvard Univ., p. 17.
[18] History of Yale College—Barnard's Jour. of Educ., V, 542, 1858.
[19] Quoted in Chase's Hist. of Dartmouth College and Hanover, N. H., p. 232.
[20] Ibid., p. 546.

taken from the subscription lists that yielded relatively large amounts to Princeton, Queen's, Brown, and William and Mary if these were extant. In these gifts there is reflected much of the simplicity of the social and economic life of that time. Actual money was scarce, as shown by the repeated issues of currency by the various Colonies, hence such gifts as Dartmouth's sawmills and blacksmith shop and Harvard's printing press entered most naturally and effectively into the making of colleges in those days.

2. USE OF THE SUBSCRIPTION METHOD.

These colleges were all active in gathering funds by the subscription plan both in England and in America. Princeton received a subscription of £1,000 proclamation, given in produce and money, in the southern Colonies in 1769, another of £1,000 from Boston in the same year, and £2,000 in England. Brown received $4,500 by subscription in England and Ireland in 1764.[21] Blair brought home from England £2,500 which he had gathered by subscription for William and Mary in 1693. Dartmouth collected £10,000 in England in 1769, while King's and Pennsylvania shared equally a subscription fund of £10,000 gathered in England. These are only the most striking instances of the use of this method of collecting the gifts of the people. Through the churches this method was repeatedly used and frequently the colonial court or the town officials would name a day on which a subscription for the college would be asked from every citizen.

3. FEW LARGE GIFTS.

In that day of small gifts a few names of great benefactors stand out. Whatever the " moiety " of Harvard's estate was, it was a princely sum in the year 1638 for a college with one or two teachers and a half dozen students.[22] This was the first great gift to education in America, and it is worthy of note that it was not tied up with conditions which might make it useless to the Harvard College of the future. It was given by request to the college outright, and constituted half of the fortune and the entire library of one of the wealthiest and most noted men in New England.

The immediate influence of this was great, and is well recorded by the historians of the college, Quincy and Peirce. During the next few decades several gifts of £100 were received, and in 1650 Richard Saltonstall, of England, gave " to the college " goods and money worth 320 pounds sterling. In 1681 Sir Matthew Holworthy bequeathed " to be disposed of by the directors as they shall judge best for the promotion of learning and promulgation of the Gospel " £1,000. The Hon. William Stoughton erected a building in 1699 which cost £1,000 Massachusetts currency. These are the large gifts of the seventeenth century, with the exception of the gift of William and Mary, of England, to the college of Virginia.

During the next century Thomas Hollis established a professorship of divinity at Harvard (1721). In his " orders " [23] he asks " that the interest of the funds be used, £10 annually for help to a needy student for the ministry—as many of these as the funds will bear." He reserves the right to sanction all appointments during his lifetime, then leaves it to the " President and Fellows of Harvard College," and asks " that none be refused on account of his belief and

---

[21] Names of the first subscribers are given in the Collections of the Rhode Island Historical Society, Vol. VII, 273.

[22] A careful discussion of the amount of this legacy is given in Quincy's History of Harvard, Vol. I, appendix I, 460.

[23] See Quincy's Harvard, Vol. I, Appendix XLII, for copy of the instrument of gift.

18   PHILANTHROPY IN AMERICAN HIGHER EDUCATION.

practice of adult baptism."[23]   The conditions which he places upon this, the first professorship established in America by private donation, are of interest. These are his words:

I order and appoint a Professor of Divinity, to read lectures in the Hall of the College unto the students; the said Professor to be nominated and appointed from time to time by the President and Fellows of Harvard College, and that the Treasurer pay to him forty pounds per annum for his service, and that when choice is made of a fitting person, to be recommended to me for my approbation, if I be yet living.[24]

In that day of fierce theological controversies these seem to be very liberal conditions.

A few years later Hollis established a professorship of mathematics and natural philosophy.   In all, his donations total over £5,000, a sum which far exceeded any single gift to education in America up to that time.   Aside from books and goods the purposes of all his gifts were stipulated, but in such general terms and, as his letters show,[25] so fully in terms of the wishes of the president and overseers, that it constitutes an example of educational philanthropy that is worthy of note.

Madam Mary Saltonstall, who bequeathed £1,000 in 1730 for educating young men " of bright parts and good diligence for service of the Christian Church ";[26] Thomas Hancock, who founded the professorship of Hebrew and other oriental languages in 1764 with a gift of £1,000; John Alford, whose executors, acting in accordance with his wish that his money should be used to aid "pious and charitable purposes," gave £1,300 to establish a professorship " of some particular science of public utility ";[27] Nicholas Boylston, who bequeathed £1,500 for the support of a professor of rhetoric in 1772; and Dr. Ezekiel Hersey, whose gift established a professorship of anatomy and physic in 1772, are other pre-revolutionary names which figure on the list of Harvard's greatest benefactors.

At the Collegiate School of Connecticut the names of Elihu Yale and Rev. Dr. George Berkeley, with gifts of £500 and £400, respectively; at the College of New Jersey the names of Tennent and Davy, of England, with a gift of over £2,000; at King's the name of Joseph Murray with a bequest of his library and his estate worth £9,000 in 1762; and at William and Mary the names of James Blair and Robert Boyle give us other instances of educational philanthropy on a liberal scale in the colonial days.

4. GIFTS FROM TOWNS, CHURCHES, AND SOCIETIES.

In addition to these gifts from private individuals there is frequent evidence of support coming from towns, churches, and societies.   In 1764 the town of Boston collected £476 by subscription, which it gave to Harvard to repair the loss occasioned by the destruction of Harvard Hall by fire.   Nine other towns made smaller contributions to the same end, while two years previously 44 towns had made contributions to the college.   Wheelock received funds from public collections taken in several eastern towns between 1762 and 1765 which were of great value to his struggling school, soon to be known as Dartmouth

---

[23] See Quincy's Harvard, Vol. I, Appendix XLII, for copy of the instrument of gift.
[24] Quincy's Harvard, Vol. I, Appendix XLII.
[25] Numerous letters from Mr. Hollis to his agent and others in the Colonies appear as appendixes in Vol. I, of Quincy's History of Harvard.
[26] Quincy, Vol. I, p. 421.
[27] Quincy, Vol. II, p. 142.

College.[28]   In the cases of Princeton, Queen's, King's, and Brown the donations from churches were large and frequent.

The Society for the Propagation of the Gospel in Foreign Parts found the colleges appropriate agencies through which to operate in the Colonies. As early as 1714 reference is made to a gift of books to the Yale library; in 1747 the society made a large donation of books to Harvard, and £100 in money in 1764.[29] From the same society King's received £500 sterling and in 1762 a library of 1,500 books. The society also assisted in getting a collection made in England which raised nearly £6,000 sterling for the college in 1762.[30] The Society for Propagating the Gospel in New England and parts adjacent gave to Harvard 1,101 volumes and £300 sterling to repair the loss of its library in 1764. The Edinburgh Society for Promoting Religious Knowledge presented Harvard with some books in 1766, and the Society for Propagating Christian Knowledge, in Scotland, gave £30 for the purchase of books in 1769.

5. GIFTS OF BOOKS, BUILDINGS, AND LAND.

It is noticeable in the early years that many gifts of books were made to the colleges. However strongly the titles of the books may suggest the religious and theological nature of higher education, in those days such gifts were of the greatest importance when both the bounds and the methods of knowledge lay almost wholly within books alone.

There is an occasional gift of a building, and frequent reference is made to gifts of land. During the colonial period Harvard received from towns and individuals over 2,000 acres;[31] Yale received over 1,000 acres, including 300 acres from the general assembly;[32] King's received 5 acres in the heart of New York City, and 34,000 acres more from the State which were lost to the college and the State as well at the close of the Revolution;[33] Dartmouth received 400 acres from proprietors of the town of Hanover;[34] the College of New Jersey received 210 acres from the town and people of Princeton; and a large portion of Queen's campus was the gift of a private citizen. Gifts of real estate were for many years of little productive value however; so the chief support had to be money or something that could be exchanged at any time.

ANALYSIS OF THE GIFTS TO FOUR OF THE COLONIAL COLLEGES.

To get at the full meaning of the philanthropy of this period, however, complete lists of all the gifts to Harvard, Yale, King's, and the College of New Jersey, four of the nine colonial colleges, have been made and appear in Tables 3, 4, 5, and 6.

Remembering that it is not the absolute amount of a gift, but rather what the gift will purchase, that measures its value, we may ask, first: What was

[28] Chase : History of Dartmouth, p. 31.

[29] The motive back of this may be seen in the following quotation, which throws some light on the denominational motives which impelled many gifts. Referring to the gift of books : "A good investment for the conformity of four graduates of the Presbyterian College at Yale, Connecticut, had been mainly effected (in 1722–23) by theological works sent to the college in 1714."   " Two Hundred Years of the S. P. G., 1701–1900," p. 799.

[30] Ibid., pp. 775, 798.

[31] Barnard's Journal, Vol. IX, 159, gives a full list of gifts of real estate.

[32] Ibid., Vol. X, 693, mentions the important gifts.

[33] A History of Columbia Univ., 1754–1904, p. 35 ff.

[34] Chase : History of Dartmouth, p. 174.

the size of the problem which philanthropy had undertaken and what did education cost?

1. SIZE OF THE COLONIAL COLLEGES.

The numbers of students attending these colleges can be judged by the number of their graduates. Harvard rarely if ever had over 100 students before the year 1700, and at no time in the colonial period did she have over 350 or 400 students, while Yale and King's had fewer still. Pennsylvania graduated in all only 135 students before 1776, Brown 60, and Dartmouth 31. The teaching staff was also small. The president's administrative duties were insignificant, his chief function being that of instructor. Before 1720 Harvard's faculty consisted of a president and from 1 to 4 tutors. At Yale the president was assisted by from 1 to 4 tutors, rarely more than 3, before the year 1755. After 1720 Harvard's faculty gradually increased to 9; Yale's to 8; and King's to 11. In the case of King's a much larger percentage were from the start of professorial rank.

Thus, judged by the size of student body and faculty, the actual work done in the colonial colleges was small, and great sums of money were not needed.

2. THE COST OF A COLLEGE EDUCATION.

The cost of a college education at Harvard in its early days is shown in an old account book for the period 1649–50 to 1659, from which it appears that for those graduating from 1653 to 1659 the total expense ranged from £30 25s. 1¼ d. to £61 11s. 8¾d., or from about $100 to about $200 for four years' residence in college.

An itemized account of a student, Thomas Graves, of the class of 1656, by quarters, shows that he paid about 32s. for tuition. His first quarter's expenses appear as follows: [35]

	Pounds.	S.	D.	Qr.
8, 10, 54 Commones and siznges------------------------	2	8	9	2
Tuition, 8 s; study, rente, and bed, 4 s; fyer and candelle 2 s------------------------		14	0	0
Fower loode of wood------------------------		17	4	0

The other three quarters' expenses were similar to this. In 1797 this cost, according to an account of Judge Daniel Appleton White, given in volume 6 of the Massachusetts Historical Society Proceedings, page 272, would have been about $480 for the four years.

Students' bills were often paid in butter, rye, malt, hog, lamb, eggs, etc. At Princeton, Maclean tells us that a student's entire expenses in 1761 were £25 6s. proclamation money.

A fairly complete account of the tuition cost at Yale, as set forth in Table 2, data for which were gathered from Dexter's Annals, shows the tuition not to have been much different at the beginning from the above account of tuition cost at Harvard a half century earlier.

---

[35] From Mass. Hist. Proc., 1860–1862, Vol. V, p. 60.

Table 2.—Cost of education at Yale College.

Date.	Tuition.	Room.	Board.	President's salary.	Salary of tutor.
	Shillings.			C. P.¹	C. P.¹
1701..	30			120	50
1704..	30				50
1712..	30			100	
1718..	30			140	
1719..		20s.	4s. 4d.		
1725..	30				
1726..	40		4s. 8d.	140	
1727..	50			212	65
1728..	50			250	60
1729..	50			300	65
1734..	50			300	65
1737..	60				
1738..	60			300	
1740..	60			320	
1742..	24				
1745..	17				
1748..	17				
1749..	20	(22 to 26 s.)			
1754..	24	3s. or 4s. 8d.			
1755..	24				
1759..	26				
1764..	30				
1767..				200	
1768..				200	(²)
1769..	48	6s.			
1777..				160	

¹ In country pay 120 equaled about £60 sterling or one-third.
² £57 6s. 8d.

At Dartmouth in 1773 tuition and board together were £20 a year. At William and Mary the tuition in 1724 was " 20s. entrance and 20s. a year for pupilage for each scholar." A woman offered to " undertake the keeping of the college table at the rate of £11 per annum for each scholar, with the other advantages allowed to Mr. Jackson." ³⁶ At Princeton tuition was £3 in 1754, £4 in 1761, £5 in 1773, and board in 1761 was £15 a year, according to Maclean.

Reference to the prices of a few well-known commodities will help one to appreciate the apparently small gifts which we are to examine. In 1641 common labor was worth 1s. 6d. per day, the next year corn was worth 2s. 6d. and wheat and barley 4s. per bushel. In 1670 wheat was worth 5s., corn 3s. ; the year following labor was worth from 1s. 3d. to 1s. 8d. In 1704 corn was worth 2s. and wheat 3s. 8d. In 1727 wheat was worth 6s. 6d. to 8s. In 1752 corn was worth 4s. and wheat 6s. In 1776 corn was 3s. and wheat 6s. 8d.³⁷

3. SALARIES OF COLLEGE PROFESSORS.

One further item of interest in this connection is the salary of the teaching staff. This was the chief item of expenditure in every college and is a fair index to the value of any gift or to the value of the funds available for the use of the college at any time. As shown in Table 2, Yale's president received from £60 to £300, while the salary of a tutor was very much less. Maclean thinks that Princeton's president did not receive over £50 annually before 1754. In that year his salary was fixed at £150 proclamation, rising to £200 proclama-

³⁶ " Proc. of Visitors of William and Mary College, 1716," in The Virginia Magazine of History and Biography, Vol. IV, p. 174.
³⁷ From Weeden's Economic and Social History of New England, 1620–1789, Vol. II.

tion in 1757 and to £400 in 1766, only to be reduced again to £250 with the usual perquisites, and finally to £200 in 1767. In 1768 it rose again to £350 proclamation, or about £206 sterling. In 1752 Maclean states the salary of a tutor to have been £20 sterling and £66 in 1767. The three professors at Princeton in 1767 received: Divinity, £175; mathematics, £150; language and logic, £125. In 1654 the overseers of Harvard College offered Rev. Mr. Charles Channing the presidency of the college at a salary of £100 per annum.[38] From Judge Sewell's diary the salary in 1698 appears to have been £200.[39]

At the close of the colonial period Harvard's president was receiving £300,[40] a professor about £200, and the librarian £60. In October, 1766, a committee of the colonial assembly of Connecticut reported that Yale ought to have:

1. A president, at £150 per annum.
2. A professor of divinity, at £113 6s. 8d. per annum.
3. A senior tutor, at £65 1s. 4d. per annum.
4. Three junior tutors, at £51 1s. 4d. per annum each.

Salaries at William and Mary were little different. President Blair, the first president, received £150 at first, and later only £100, increasing in 1755 to £200. During the same period a professor received £80 and fees of 20s. per student. In 1729 each professor received £150, but no fees.[41] In 1770 the president received £200, each of two divinity professors £200, two other professors each £100, master of grammar school £150, first usher £75, second usher £40.[42]

When one considers that the entire expenditures of Harvard for the year 1777 were but £1,086 18s. 2d. and that the college had but £386 18s. 2d. to pay it with, the residue being paid " by assessments on the scholars for study-rent, tuition, and other necessary charges, amounting *communibus annis* to about £700;[43] or that the average annual income of William and Mary College during the decade 1754 to 1764 was £1,936 14s. 6¾d.,[44] these salaries appear relatively high.

THE FUNCTION OF PHILANTHROPY IN THE COLLEGES.

What now is the character of the educational philanthropy which was practiced in the midst of these conditions? Was it constructive, or did it follow tradition? It might be hard to answer these questions to our entire satisfaction, but an examination of the parts of Tables 3, 4, 5, and 6, which refer to this period, will throw light on the subject.

---

[38] Quincy: Vol. I, Appendix IV.
[39] Ibid., Vol. I, Appendix XI, p. 490.
[40] Ibid., Vol. II, p. 241.
[41] Tyler, pp. 137, 144.
[42] Tyler quoted these amounts from the college bursar's books, Williamsburg, the Old Colonial Capitol, p. 158.
[43] Quincy: Vol. II, p. 241.
[44] Tyler, Lyon G., " Williamsburg, the Old Colonial Capital," p. 156.

TABLE 3.—*Donations and grants to Harvard University, 1636–1910—Distribution of the donations by individuals.*[1]

Dates.	Total donations by individuals.	Per cent of all gifts from England.	Total grant by colony.	Per cent of total donations by individuals given to—								Per cent in form of—	
				General fund.	Purpose specified.	Present use.	Permanent endowment.	Pious and indigent students.	Professorships.	Fellowships and scholarships.	Library.	Gift.	Bequest.
1636–1640..	$1,936	......	$2,002	99	1	100	......	......	......	......	......	......	100
1641–1645..	4,826	19	....	60	40	91	9	......	......	9	31	100	......
1646–1650..	333	......	445	100	......	......	100	......	......	......	......	......	100
1651–1655..	1,475	......	666	27	73	88	22	......	......	......	18	100	......
1656–1660..	6,785	12	1,665	79	21	85	15	15	......	......	1	61	39
1661–1665..	266	63	....	37	63	100	......	63	......	......	......	90	10
1666–1670..	4,754	9	66	36	64	36	64	......	63	......	......	100	......
1671–1675..	7,745	6	1,831	.5	99.5	99.5	.5	.5	......	......	......	99.5	.5
1676–1680..	900	42	1,665	82	18	100	......	......	......	18	33	67
1681–1685..	7,041	34	1,998	75	25	100	......	......	......	25	30	70
1686–1690..	2,558	......	1,665	100	......	87	13	13	......	......	......	......	100
1691–1695..	462	......	1,332	100	......	100	......	......	......	......	3	97
1696–1700..	3,724	......	1,831	10	90	100	......	......	......	......	100	......
1701–1705..	1,498	......	....	89	11	100	......	......	(²)	......	11	89
1706–1710..	1,232	32	2,337	13	87	100	......	50	......	......	54	46
1711–1715..	2,979	70	2,758	11	89	88	22	......	......	......	77	23
1716–1720..	9,171	11	11,107	30	60	25	75	37	......	7	90	10
1721–1725..	8,259	15	907	75	25	39	61	12	25	4	9	90	10
1726–1730..	5,153	53	4,485	26	74	40	60	25	33	25	2	75	25
1731–1735..	2,496	80	2,354	60	40	46	54	17	35	......	97	3
1736–1740..	2,643	37	654	9	91	48	52	11	44	12	......	77	23
1741–1745..	2,973	78	378	3	97	97	3	......	3	......	100	......
1746–1750..	1,277	78	942	16	84	83	17	......	12	......	3	97
1751–1755..	1,112	90	9,459	9	91	81	19	......	......	......	100
1756–1760..	2,584	77	2,946	38	62	79	21	2	20	......	47	53
1761–1765..	17,397	13	35,507	42	58	46	54	......	23	......	1	3	97
1766–1770..	6,336	17	14,162	13	87	100	......	......	49	97	3
1771–1775..	12,989	27	6,594	14	86	10	90	......	64	.7	19	35	65
1776–1780..	1,814	......	3,203	44	56	100	......	......	66	44
1781–1785..	1,800	......	4,878	3	97	14	86	80	......	4	......	40	60
1786–1790..	7,905	......	3,220	......	100	58	42	......	42	......	58	42
1791–1795..	9,163	......	....	100	......	100	......	79	......	100
1796–1800..	4,000	......	....	100	87.5	12.5	......	12	87	12	88
1801–1805..	33,333	......	....	100	6	94	......	94	......	100	......
1806–1810..	5,444	......	....	100	8	92	......	......	8	......	100
1811–1815..	47,333	......	20,000	......	100	1	99	.7	99	......	53	47
1816–1820..	76,700	......	50,000	5	95	15	85	......	36	12	52	48
1821–1825..	60,003	......	30,000	3	97	17	83	2	76	16	26	74
1826–1830..	145,652	......	....	66	34	1	99	......	21	.6	29	71
1831–1835..	44,951	......	....	100	14	86	2.	44	14	14	86
1836–1840..	31,180	......	....	100	10	90	6	16	......	93	7
1841–1845..	303,702	......	....	4	96	25	75	.1	......	15	9	37	63
1846–1850..	205,383	......	....	2	98	43	57	......	1	.2	52	48
1851–1855..	131,898	......	....	100	58	42	......	29	12	4	39	61
1856–1860..	254,713	......	....	12	88	38	62	......	8	.2	11	62	38
1861–1865..	³680,917	......	....	2	88	7	93	.7	.2	2	3	29	71
1866–1870..	³254,741	......	....	22	78	9	91	.3	......	14	23	96	4
1871–1875..	773,427	......	....	7	93	64	36	......	6	8	75	25
1876–1880..	784,541	......	....	5	95	16	84	3	12	8	7	51	49
1881–1885..	1,487,508	......	....	17	83	22	78	.3	8	3.5	12	66	33
1886–1890..	2,594,554	......	....	21	79	23	77	......	.03	5	16	24	76
1891–1895..	1,586,855	......	....	22	78	29	71	......	3	10.8	4	45	55
1896–1900..	4,306,609	......	....	26	74	52	48	6	11	5	1.5	43	57
1901–1905..	7,648,309	......	....	14	86	36	64	1.8	8	3.5	1.4	79	21
1906–1910..	7,309,950	......	....	13	87	20	80	.2	9	9	3.4	64	36

[1] These data were compiled from three sources mainly. Those before 1851 were taken from Quincy's History of Harvard University, 2 vols., published in 1840, and from the lists of "Grants and Donations to Harvard College" published in Barnard's American Journal of Education, Vol. IX, pp. 139–160, Sept., 1860. Those for the years 1852–1910 were taken from the annual reports of the president and treasurer of Harvard College.

² Gift of 27 acres of land, income to be used for scholarships for students from town of Dorchester.

³ Data for the years 1862–63 and 1867–68 are not included.

TABLE 4.—*Donations and grants to Yale University, 1701–1900—Distribution of donations by individuals.*[1]

Dates.	Total grants by colony.	Total donations by individuals.	General fund.	Specified purposes.	Present use.	Permanent endowment.	Religious purposes.	Scientific purposes.	Professorships.	Fellowship and scholarships.	Pious and indigent students.	Library.	Gift.	Bequest.
				Per cent of total donations by individuals given to—									Per cent in form of—	
1701–1705.	$1,335	$134		100	100							100	100	
1706–1710.	1,335													
1711–1715.	3,627	1,424		100	100								100	
1716–1720.	1,758	5,416	87	13	100							12	100	
1721–1725.	4,005	868	51	49	100								100	
1726–1730.	2,203	1,971		100	100							100	100	
1731–1735.	2,448	13,608[2]		100	1	99		14.5		99			100	
1736–1740.	2,997	67		100	100			52				50	100	
1741–1745.	2,679	352	19	81	29	71			80				50	50
1746–1750.	5,233	53	80	20	100			37				16	100	
1751–1755.	4,520	159		100	11	89	89			89		10	100	
1756–1760.		968		100	82	18	97	13	18				100	
1761–1765.	1,460	1,041		100	100		82	0.5				5	90	10
1766–1770.	3,595	109	89	11	100							10	100	
1771–1775.	1,282	62		100	100								100	
1776–1780.		1,290	73	27	100								80	20
1781–1785.		3,233	50	50	50	50							50	50
1786–1790.		1,458		100	100			22	1				100	
1791–1795.	40,629	1,122		100		100						8		100
1796–1800.												100		
1801–1805.														
1806–1810.		2,000		100		100						100	100	
1811–1815.	8,785													
1816–1820.		6,000	100		100								50	50
1821–1825.		78,848	2	98	30	70	58	20	50	15	1	3	98	2
1826–1830.	7,000	14,664	3	97	75	25	6	3	21	2		34	100	
1831–1835.		126,138	30	70	32	68		1				3	97.3	1.7
1836–1840.		12,000		100	17	83					16	83	18	82
1841–1845.		38,100		100	31	69			66				100	
1846–1850.		15,850	25	75	27	71				8		34	44	56
1851–1855.		177,490	21	79	95	5	30	9		5			95	5
1856–1860.		329,500		100	58	42	40	60		24	6		92	
1861–1865.		434,648	2	98	53	47	21	6	44	4			97	3
1866–1870.		743,481		94	62	38	11	17	9		0.5	2	92	8
1871–1875.		1,135,007	15	85	89	11	42	24	11	5	.3	2	93	7
1876–1880.		417,000	33	66	45	55	5	2	28	3	4	4	46	54
1881–1885.		623,200	53	47	98	20	21	28	2	1.5		1.5	85	15
1886–1890.		3,349,471	1	99	92	8	6	13	1		3	5	18	82
1891–1895.		1,553,382	21	79	74	26	10	26	5	10	1	3		
1896–1900.		1,729,094	35	65	81	19	3	8	15	3	.5	4		

[1] Sources for this table: Conn. Colonial Records; Dexter—Yale Biographies and Annals, 1701; Steiner—Hist. of Educ. in Conn.; Bagg—Four Years at Yale; Stile's Diary, Vol. III; Trumbull—Hist. of Conn. Vol. II; Papers of New Haven Hist. Soc.; Kingsley—Yale Book; Baldwin—Hist. of Yale College; and reports of the president and treasurer of Yale College.

[2] £3,000 of this was the value of a farm which the college leased for 999 years, and though now worth $140,000, brings the university only $145 per year. New Haven Hist. Soc. Papers, Vol. I, p. 156.

TABLE 5.—*Donations and grants to Princeton University, 1745–1856 and 1906–1910—Distribution of the donations by individuals.*[1]

| | | | Per cent of total donations by individuals given to— | | | | | | | | | | | Given in form of— | |
Dates.	Total donations by individuals.	Total grants by Colony.	General funds.	Specified purpose.	Present use.	Permanent endowment.	Professorships.	Fellowships and scholarships.	Library.	Pious and indigent students.	Plant.	Religious purposes.	Scientific purposes.	Gift.	Bequest.
1745–1750	$3,953		100		100					25	67	25		99	1
1751–1755	16,261		1	99	100								5	100	
1756–1760	973		100		100				(²)	100		100		100	
1761–1765		(³)													
1766–1770	7,058		92	8	79	21	6			1		8		99	1
1771–1775	146			100	100							100		100	
1776–1780	3,300		100		100					63		93			100
1781–1785	1,550		6	94	69	31				63		93		31	69
1786–1790	3,657		10	90	18	82				90		81		9	91
1791–1795	10,677			100	100						100				100
1796–1800	80	$8,010			100		100	100				100		100	
1801–1805	53,278		1	99	99			2	1		1		5	98	2
1806–1810	13,500		3	97	3	97	55			16	82	96		96	4
1811–1815	3,480			100	88	12	12			17		97		88	12
1816–1820	3,080			100	98	2	2			98		97		100	
1821–1825	9,080			100	33	67	1	66		33		33		100	
1826–1830	17,030		3	97	27	73	70			15		11	.5	100	
1831–1835	4,785			100	99	1	1			44	27	62	6	75	25
1836–1840	3,185			100	98	2	2			60		97		98	2
1841–1845	6,080			37	63	99	1	1		37		49		63	37
1846–1850	3,540			100	98	2	2			54		98		100	
1851–1855	105,080			100	8	90	1	95		3		3		100	
1906–1910	4,759,115		23	77	15	85		4	1			.01	5	87	13

[1] Data for this table were taken from Maclean's Hist. of the College of New Jersey; Murray's Hist. of the college; and from reports of the president and treasurer of the college.
[2] In 1860 the library contained about 12,000 volumes, practically all of which had been donated. See Maclean, Hist. of the College of New Jersey, Vol. I, p. 206.
[3] Right to conduct lottery.

There were three sources of income for the colleges: The general court, philanthropy, and student fees. In the accompanying tables we are concerned with that of philanthropy mainly, though for comparative purposes, column 1 gives the amounts received from the State.

The gifts are grouped into five-year periods. Column 2 gives us a picture of the stream of donations that has been flowing for so many years into the treasuries of four of our oldest colleges.

The first large grouping of the gifts is that which shows them to have been given to the college unconditionally on the one hand, or with certain conditions which wholly or in part determine how the money shall be spent on the other. The next grouping is that which states whether the gift is for present use or for permament endowment. Further than this it is a question of just what is the specific condition. Is it for the library, for scholarships, for apparatus, etc.?

FUNCTION OF THE STATE IN HIGHER EDUCATION.

During the eighteenth century Harvard received relatively much more from the State than in the seventeenth century. Yet during the entire colonial period the loss of that support would have been almost fatal to the college. The same

TABLE 6.—Donations and grants to Columbia University, 1754–1910—Distributions of the donations by individuals.[1]

Dates.	Total donations by individuals.	Total grants by colony.	Per cent of total donations by individuals given to—								In form of—	
			General fund.	Specified purpose.	Present use.	Permanent endowment.	Pious and indigent students.	Professorships.	Fellowships and scholarships.	Library.	Gift.	Bequest.
1750–1755		$21,593										
1756–1760	$115,828	27,580									29	71
1761–1765	38,466	4,860									99	1
1766–1770												
1771–1775												
1776–1780												
1781–1785	4,860	12,462										100
1786–1790		4,860										
1791–1795		48,600										
1796–1800		11,935										
1801–1805		8,958										
1806–1810		2,700										
1811–1815												
1816–1820		10,000										
1821–1825												
1826–1830												
1831–1835												
1836–1840												
1841–1845	20,000			100		100		100				100
1846–1850												
1851–1855	1,000			100		100					13	87
1856–1860	1,150		87	13	100						28	72
1861–1865	2,800			100	28	72		72			100	
1866–1870	200			100	100						100	
1871–1875	4,300			100	100						100	
1876–1880	10,000			100	40	60			50		40	60
1881–1885	18,945		5	95	37	63			63		95	5
1886–1890	247,911		40	60	9	91			14	34	31	69
1891–1895	4,974,385		8	92	82	18			3	22	93	7
1896–1900	3,530,160		0.3	99.7	44	56		6	2.5	35	68	32
1901–1905	3,910,570		3.0	97	51	49		12	0.6	2	92	8
1906–1910	4,382,015		26	74	52	48	0.2	15	2.4	1.5	75	25

[1] The data for this table were taken from an official publication of the university entitled "Columbia University—Gifts and Endowments—1754–1904," and from the reports of the treasurer of the university covering the years subsequent to 1904. This covers the Columbia Corporation alone and does not include Barnard and Teachers' Colleges.

is true of Yale and Columbia. For Princeton, however, there is a different story. Only once during the colonial period was any aid given by the State to Princeton. In 1762 the assembly granted the right to hold a lottery for an amount not to exceed £5,000.[45] This was very real help, and since it involved a special act of the legislature it is fair to assume that it shows friendliness on the part of the State. A few years after this period closes, the State granted to the college £600 annually for three years, to be paid in quarterly payments.[46] In the report of the committee which represented the college before the legislature it appears that legislators raised the objection that the institution was under the "sole and exclusive control of one denomination of Christians." The difficulties with which this act was passed and the result of the act show the extent to which the College of New Jersey was not a State institution.

[45] Murray : Hist. of Educ. in New Jersey, p. 27.
[46] Maclean, Vol. I, p. 13, gives a copy of the report of a committee appointed to apply to the State for aid.

It is said on good authority, declares Maclean, that not one of the legislators who voted for the act was returned to his office at the ensuing election, so bitter was the feeling against the act.[47]

It is to be remembered that New Jersey, unlike Connecticut and Massachusetts, was settled by people of several different religious sects, and that while religious education of the Congregational type practically meant State education for Yale and Harvard, it meant only church education for the New Jersey college.[48]

A more careful study of the problem of higher education and the State is inviting, but a few illustrations to show that State education of collegiate grade, while understood and practiced in part, was not a fully established educational social philosophy in the colonial days, serves our purpose. Wheelock's Indian school received aid, £50 per annum for five years, once from the Colony of New Hampshire, and after the school became Dartmouth College it received aid of £60 in 1771 and £500 in 1773, after which no formal request was ever made, though one was prepared in 1775.[49] New Hampshire apparently had no thought of Dartmouth as a State institution.

The College of Rhode Island was essentially a denominational school established in a State where the Baptist faith predominated but by the church of that denomination in several Colonies. There should theoretically have been no hindrance to making their college quite as much an object of State concern as was the case with Yale, Harvard, and Kings; but the facts show that little help was ever received by the college from the Colony, due, no doubt, to Rhode Island's insistence upon a real separation of church and state.

At William and Mary the relation of college and state varied with the governors of the province, several of whom were exceedingly unfriendly to higher education in general, and to President Blair and his college in particular. But in spite of these the college received much genuine assistance from the Colony. At the outset it was granted a duty on liquors imported, and on skins and furs exported, which by October, 1695, amounted to £441 sterling,[50] and " upwards of 3,000 pounds *communibus annis.*"[51] In 1718 a grant of £1,000 was made by the Colony to establish three scholarships (part of this fund was invested in negro slaves). In 1726 a grant of £200 annually for 21 years was made from the duty on liquors. In 1734 this increased to include the entire income of the 1 penny per gallon duty on liquors, providing that part of the money should be used for the purchase of books, each of which was to bear a label, reading " The gift of the General Assembly of Virginia in the Year 1734."[52] In 1759 the college received another grant in the form of a tax on peddlers. Without making the list exhaustive, it is evident that the State took an interest in the college and bore a fairly substantial part of its financial burdens, even if it did not assume the real responsibility.

CONDITIONAL AND UNCONDITIONAL GIFTS.

In the case of Harvard there seems to have been a gradual and fairly persistent tendency for people to specify how the college should use their gifts. At Yale there was somewhat of a general tendency toward unconditional gifts,

---

[47] Maclean, Vol. I, p. 18.
[48] During and following the Revolution Yale could not get help from the State for much the same reason. The legislature demanded that " civilians " be placed on the board of trustees before the State rendered aid. This was finally done.
[49] Chase, pp. 272, 277.
[50] Bruce, Philip Alexander: Institutional History of Virginia in the Seventeenth Century, Vol. I, p. 395.
[51] Howe's History of the Colony of Virginia, p. 325.
[52] This is another evidence that the State did not consider the college a State institution.

but most of the early gifts were conditional. At Princeton also there was a tendency to place some condition upon the gifts, and with the emphasis in the early years somewhat between that for Yale, which emphasizes conditional and that for Harvard which emphasizes unconditional gifts.

In the early days a college was just one thing. It was a teaching institution only and there was little occasion for giving other than " to the college." Yet many gifts were carefully safeguarded with conditions.

A glance at the succeeding columns of the tables, however, and an explanation of some of the large figures in the " purpose specified " column will suffice to show that the main current, even of the conditional gifts, was generally in line with the fundamental aim and practical needs of the college. Taking the 73 per cent in the " purpose specified " column of the Harvard table, the explanation is simply £60 worth of books and £251 15s. 6d. toward " the repairs of the college." The 99.5 per cent in 1671–1675 is largely accounted for by the contributions from 44 towns " for the erection of a new building for the college," amounting to over £2,000. The 90 per cent in 1696–1700 is mostly accounted for by the cost of Stoughton Hall, built and presented to the college by the Hon. William Stoughton in 1699. The first 100 per cent in the " purpose specified " column of the Princeton table was gifts to the aid of pious and indigent students, a very common mode of assistance in those days, as it is now in many colleges. In the Yale table the first 100 per cent refers to books for the library, and the second to nearly 1,000 volumes, mostly from England.

GIFTS FOR PRESENT USE AND FOR ENDOWMENT.

The next general grouping of the funds is into those for present use and those for permanent endowment. It is very noticeable that all through this period the gifts were in the main to be used at once by the college. The " dead hand," good or bad, plays little part in this period of our educational history. The 100 per cent in the Harvard table, " permanent endowment " column, 1646–1650, was just one bequest, and that to the college in general. The 64 per cent in 1666–1670 was for the establishment of " two fellows and two scholars." The 75 per cent in 1716–1730 was for the maintenance of preachers and for the education of pious young men for the ministry, both entirely appropriate to the needs of Harvard at that time. This same tendency appears to have been true for the other colleges.

HOW GIFTS WERE CONDITIONED.

What and how many kinds of restrictions were placed upon these gifts? From the very start there are restricted gifts, at first few in number, and falling within the main object of the college, but gradually increasing in number and variety until in the present day they are extremely numerous. During the period under discussion, however, they were few in number. They are for buildings, for the library, for aid of pious and indigent students, for scholarships and fellowships, for equipment, and for professorships.

INFLUENCE OF CONDITIONAL GIFTS UPON THE GROWTH OF THE COLLEGE.

To what extent do these restricted gifts tend to broaden the purpose and function of the college? There can be cited numerous instances of where an entirely new field of work has been undertaken by a college as the result of such a gift. Observatories, scientific schools, hospitals, and botanical gardens are common illustrations of this. In the colonial days, however, when the economic and social life was restricted; when for the most part professional life meant the ministry, and a ministry whose profession rested upon accepted truths and philosophies long ago written down in books, and not upon ability and training in the discovery of new truth and the making of new creeds; when all learning was book learning; we expect the conditions placed upon benefactions to reflect these ideas and conditions.

To say that "endowment" has not produced an educational experiment until it has completely departed from the common aims and ideas of people in general, however, is to restrict the meaning of educational experiment. The founding of a professorship of divinity in 1721 was an experiment in a way, even though theology was then the center of the college curriculum. If this professorship did nothing startling by way of educational experimentation, it at least shifted the emphasis in the Harvard curriculum, which means that it made Harvard a slightly different Harvard from what it had been.

So, while an examination of the tables shows that nothing very unusual was started by gifts during this period, it also shows that without the gifts the colleges would have been different from what they were.

A study of the gifts "to pious and indigent students" is especially interesting. Yale seems to have received nothing for this purpose before 1825. The same is not true, however, for either Harvard or Princeton. The fact that the tendency to add to these funds to-day, and that they are of such large consequence in our theological colleges particularly, gives us a special interest in the early ancestry of this particular kind of beneficence. We can not help noting the absence of such funds in our modern scientific schools. To say that our present research fellowship is the same thing is not true. Competitive scholarships and fellowships are very old methods of helping students and not in any way connected with the funds here considered. In colonial times the condition almost always read "for the benefit of pious and indigent students of the gospel ministry," or words to that effect. Since a large percentage of colonial college students were training for the ministry,[53] it is perhaps unfair to assume that indigence was regarded as a virtue or proper qualification for entering that profession. The income of a minister was about equal to that of a professor, so the economic outlook for the theological student could scarcely be responsible for the ministry calling its members largely from the indigent class. Whatever the explanation, it seems a fact that colonial Harvard and Princeton did subsidize a class of students who classified as "indigent, pious, and desirous of entering the ministry."

The plan of establishing scholarships and fellowships, granted on basis of scholarship and general ability, appears first at Harvard in 1643, with a gift of £100 from Lady Moulson, of England. There were very few such funds established in the colonial period, but there were enough to show that the idea, old in Europe of course, had been brought into the colonial college.

The gifts for the establishment of professorships, usually regarded as on the whole the most useful of all conditional benefactions to higher education,[54] have played some part in the development of our colleges since the first gift for that purpose in 1721, when the Hollis professorship of divinity was established at Harvard. From then on these gifts take a prominent place among Harvard's benefactions, and there are a few such gifts to Yale and Princeton. Table 7 will show, in order of their establishment, the kinds of professorships which were established in this period, the field of work each covered, and how each was endowed.

---

[53] See "Professional Distribution of College and University Graduates," by Bailey B. Burritt, U. S. Bu. of Educ. Bul., 1912, No. 19.

[54] See President Eliot's An. Rep. of Harvard Univ., 1901–2, p. 61.

TABLE 7.—*Distribution and character of pre-Revolutionary professorships.*

Dates.	Field of work to be covered.	How endowed.	Place.	Founding gift.
1721	Divinity.....................	Gift by Thos. Hollis..........	Harvard......	Income £40 annually.
1727	Mathematics and natural philosophy.	Gift by Thos. Hollis..........	Harvard......	£390 sterling.
1754	Divinity.....................	Gift by Philip Livingston....	Yale..........	£28½ sterling.
1764	Hebrew and other oriental languages.	Bequest by Thos. Hancock...	Harvard......	£1,000 sterling.
1766	Divinity.....................	Gift by Jno. Williams........	Princeton.....	£100 sterling.
1771	Rhetoric and oratory........	Bequest by Nicholas Boylston	Harvard......	£1,500 sterling.

Here are six professorships—three of which are divinity and two others more or less allied to divinity, four founded by bequest and two by gift, all but one on a fair foundation and that one soon enlarged by subscription— founded in the half century preceding the Revolution, which, when considered in the light of the small faculties of that time, represent a very substantial accomplishment for philanthropy. The fields covered by these professorships were all entirely legitimate, in fact essential to the meaning of a college at that time. We must not overlook the fact, however, that such a gift was not made at Harvard during almost its first century of work, at Yale during its first half century, and at Princeton for 20 years. The precedent for founding professorships is, of course, very old in Europe, and it is a bit surprising that such endowments were begun so late in the Colonies.

The endowment of the library is scarcely second in importance to that of professorships. The column representing gifts to the library is only partially complete, since so many of the gifts were in books and manuscripts, the value of which was only occasionally to be found. The money gifts to libraries during this period, including gifts of books when value was stated, were more prominent in Yale than in Harvard or Princeton.

THE FORM OF GIFTS.

The form of the gift varies somewhat with the college, but in all the larger percentage of benefactions for this period are by direct gift instead of by bequest. This is slightly so for Harvard, more so for Princeton, and pronouncedly so for Yale. The bequests are more often presented for permanent rather than for immediate use, though they have not been segregated here to show this.

IMPORTANCE OF GIFTS FROM ENGLAND.

Before passing from this period some note should be taken of the important part which the mother country played in providing money for the infant colleges in this country. Evidence for this is shown for Harvard only. From these figures, however, it is evident that the colonial colleges had many friends in the mother country. In fact, without these gifts it is hard to say what might have been the fate of colonial Harvard.

English donations did not come through the avenues of the church and religious societies alone, though religious motives are often evident in the conditions adhering to the gifts, which were for the aid of library, professorships, indigent students, etc.

When war broke down the friendly feeling between the two countries this remarkable source of support, valuable in more ways than one, rapidly dried up. It is frequently pointed out that the beginning of our national period is the ending of English and the beginning of French influence in our higher education. So it is, and the ending of the column of figures here referred to is a concrete statement of one of ·the things that is meant by the ending of the English influence.

When we consider these figures in the light of the developments which the gifts opened up and the suggestions they brought to our colleges, ·we have more than a word picture of this transition stage in one of our higher institutions of learning.

There is one table (Table 6) not yet referred to, dealing with King's College, later Columbia University. The fact that this college received so little by way of donations through this period, and a fairly regular amount from the Colony, makes it a marked exception. This study is dealing with philanthropy, and not with the lack of it, and can only pass this with the suggestion that the political life of New York, the religious restrictions attaching to the foundation of the college, and the general and growing attitude of unfriendliness which the people felt toward the English church, and also the English Government, made it more difficult for the people to sympathize with the college and treat it as an institution of the people. Without attempting to analyze the cause further, it must be referred to here as a marked exception to the rule of college building in colonial America; and in view of the fact that gifts for other colleges not infrequently came from people in New York, we can only infer that the people themselves were not neglectful of higher education, but only of this college.

SUMMARY AND CONCLUSIONS.

This concludes a description of the educational philanthropy of the colonial period. If we were to try to characterize it briefly, we should say that, in the light of the economic conditions under which a group of young colonies were forming, it was extensive and that it was consciously focused upon a vital social problem. We should say that organized religion dominated practically all the colleges and a large proportion of the gifts, and often denominationalism tried to bend the college in this or that direction, most often with little ill effect. We should say that there is good evidence that a very large percentage of the gifts were solicited, usually for a specific purpose, and that therefore the conditions of many gifts were actually determined by the college authorities themselves, which argues that, after all, the colleges did not take form to a very marked extent in terms of the ideas, or v·' ims either, of philanthropists. We should say that the restricted gifts which ..ent to the colleges were focused in reasonable proportion upon the fundamental needs of the schools, such, for instance, as buildings and grounds (not shown separately in the tables), professorships, library, and scholarships. We should say that the unrestricted gifts, though in relative amount they varied for the three colleges, show a substantial and fairly dependable source of support for each, and that the tendency to give for immediate needs was as commendable as it was pronounced, when we realize the limited resources of the colleges.

We should say also that there is evidence in the foundation documents and facts pertaining to the actual establishing of the colleges that they were all—William and Mary a partial exception—intended from the start.to rest upon philanthropy, and that the important service of philanthropy was not in its money and property gifts alone, but in responsibility borne and service rendered, service which meant not only self-sacrifice to a cause but constructive thinking and planning.

While the colonial governments rendered most important service to William and Mary, Yale, Harvard, and King's, though not to Princeton, Brown, Dartmouth, and Rutgers, it does not appear that in any case the Colony frankly and fully accepted the responsibility for developing a college. State aid to higher education was an accepted fact when we think of Massachusetts, Connecticut, Virginia, and New York, but not elsewhere. And in these cases there are explanations to be made which do not fully justify our calling any of them State institutions in the present accepted sense.

If there is in this a lesson for modern philanthropy, it is in the persistence with which the gifts flowed into the colleges under all circumstances, and the simple and sane directions under which these gifts did their work.

Chapter III.
THE EARLY NATIONAL PERIOD, 1776–1865.

The treatment of the years 1776 to 1865 as one period in the history of educational philanthropy is a more or less arbitrary division of time in the nature, extent, or methods of giving during these years. Yet there are some reasons, aside from convenience, for studying these first 90 years of our national existence as a single period.

As was pointed out above, the gifts from England practically ceased at the time of the Revolution. The Colonies now became independent States, and began to face grave social and political responsibilities. Not only were the ties with the mother country broken, but new, and for future educational development, significant friendships were formed in Europe with peoples whose educational ideas and institutions were quite unlike those of England. In losing this important source of support and influence, in forming new political and, as it proved, educational ties in Europe, and in facing her new political future, all American institutions enter upon a new period and must learn to function in new terms.

Once a Nation was established, its next great political crisis was in 1861. During these years there had been remarkable political and industrial achievements, important religious movements, an unheard-of expansion of population to the west, and numerous and varied social philosophies had been tried out and proved failures in practice.

All these movements and ideas were more or less reflected in the development of higher education. There had been a decline in interest in education, succeeded by an educational revival; there had been a rapid growth in the number of colleges; the Nation and the States had shown an interest in education by the ordinances of 1785 and 1787 and by the actual founding of several State colleges. It is mainly to philanthropy, however, that we must look as the chief agency in the development of the American college during these first 90 years of our national life. To trace the development of colleges through these years, and to describe the part which philanthropy played, is the problem of this chapter.

THE NUMBER OF COLLEGES AND HOW STARTED.

So far as mere numbers of institutions are concerned, private giving bore the larger part of the responsibility for higher learning during the early years. The States took no very definite step before 1794, and then in most cases followed rather tardily the lead of private and church-endowed colleges. What the States did, however, was not insignificant. From the foundation of Harvard down they had contributed liberally to higher education.[1]

While making an occasional grant upon request from a college is different from taking full responsibility, yet we must remember two things: First, States were themselves in process of making and had no traditions or precedents to follow in such matters; second, private and church-endowed education had centuries of precedent and traditions to point the way. In other words, society had been accustomed to using the church and private agencies for handling its college problems, and it is not surprising that it was slow in placing that function upon the State.

During this period, then, one may say that the ideas of State support and control of higher education worked themselves out, but that the chief burden rested upon private and church donations.

This is brought out still more clearly in Table 8, which shows the names of all the States added to the original 13 during this period, the dates of their admission, the name, date, and source of control of the first college established in each, the date when the State college or university was founded, and the number of colleges which had been founded in each State before the State university was established.

There are 23 States in this group, and in only 2, Nevada and Florida, was the State university the first institution of higher education founded. In three others, however, the State and a privately endowed school were started in the same year. A comparison of the date columns in the table will show that in most cases the State was more than 10 years old before it established a State college or university. This was doubtless due in most cases to the fact that the State was already well supplied with colleges, as appears from the next to the last column in the table. One other set of facts in this table is of interest, viz, the control of these colleges. In nearly every case it was the church which did the pioneering. Those marked nonsectarian were usually none the less religious projects, and some of them so marked were originally denominational.

Philanthropy, for the most part through the church, is therefore not only responsible from the standpoint of mere numbers of colleges throughout this period, but also for the actual college pioneering of the ever-broadening frontier of the new country.

---

[1] Williams College (1793) received State grants as follows: 1789, lottery for £1,200, building for free school: 1793, £1,200; in 1816, three-sixteenths of the Massachusetts bank tax for 10 years, equaling $30,000; in 1859 a moiety of money from sale of Back Bay lands, $25,000, last grant in 1868, $75,000. Colby College (1813) (Maine was then part of Massachusetts) received State grants as follows from Massachusetts: In 1813 a township of land, and again in 1815 a township of land; from Maine, in 1821, $1,000 a year for 7 years (to reduce tuition fees); 1825, $1,000 annually for three years; 1829, $1,000; 1832, $1,000 (one-half to help indigent students); 1861, two half townships of land on condition that college raise $21,000 by Apr. 1, 1863; in 1903, $15,000 to rebuild (after fire). Amherst College (1821), in 1827, in 1831, in 1832, 1838, and in 1839, requests refused; in 1847, $25,000 granted. Bowdoin College (1802), in 1794, five townships of land; in 1820, $1,500 plus $1,000 annually "until the legislature shall otherwise direct"; in 1820 also $3,000 annually for seven years, beginning 1824.

TABLE 8.—*Date of establishment and sources of support and control of the first college or university in each of the States admitted before 1865.*

States.	Date admitted.	First college.		Control.	State university founded.	Colleges founded before State university.
		Name.	Date established.			
Kentucky	1792	Transylvania University	1798	Nonsectarian	1865	11
Vermont	1791	Middlebury College	1800	....do	1800	0
Tennessee	1796	Tusculum College	1794	....do	1794	0
Ohio	1802	Marietta College	1800	....do	1808	1
Louisiana	1812	Jefferson College	1832	Roman Catholic	1860	4
Indiana	1816	Vincennes University	1806	Nonsectarian	1824	1
Mississippi	1817	Mississippi College	1826	Baptist	1848	2
Illinois	1818	Shurtleff College	1827	....do	1868	21
Alabama	1819	Spring Hill College	1830	Roman Catholic	1831	1
Maine	1820	Bowdoin College	1802	Nonsectarian	1868	2
Missouri	1821	St. Louis University	1818	Roman Catholic	1847	4
Arkansas	1836	Arkansas College	1872	Presbyterian	1872	0
Michigan	1837	Kalamazoo College	1833	Baptist	1841	1
Florida	1845				1887	0
Iowa	1846	Iowa Wesleyan College	1842	Methodist	1869	13
Texas	1845	Baylor University	1845	Baptist	1876	6
Wisconsin	1848	Carroll College	1846	Presbyterian	1848	2
California	1850	{College of the Pacific	1851	Methodist	} 1869	5
		{University of Santa Clara	1851	Roman Catholic		
Minnesota	1858	Hamline University	1854	Methodist	1869	4
Oregon	1859	Pacific University	1854	Congregational	1870	5
Kansas	1861	St. Mary's College	1848	Roman Catholic	1863	4
West Virginia	1863	Bethany College	1841	Disciples	1868	1
Nevada	1864				1886	....

THE BEGINNINGS.

During the Revolution higher education received a brief setback, but soon showed a tendency to keep pace with the growth of the population. The story of the beginnings of practically all the colleges founded during this period is one of penury. They were not launched with large foundation gifts or grants, such as were common at the close of the century, but most often by small gifts collected by subscription, as the following illustrations plainly show:

Williams College, founded in 1793, grew out of a free school established in 1755 by a bequest from Col. Ephraim Williams.[2]

Bowdoin College, founded in 1794, received its first important gift of $1,000 and 1,000 acres of land, worth 2 shillings an acre, from Mr. Bowdoin.

Middlebury College, founded in 1800, started with $4,000, made up of small donations from the citizens of the town of Middlebury.

Amherst College, founded in 1821, began as an academy started by a subscription in 1812 and as a college with a subscription of $52,244, known as the charity fund.

Oberlin College, founded in 1833 as one of the manual-labor projects, started with a gift of 500 acres of land, worth about $1.50 per acre, supplemented by the usual subscription plan.

Mount Holyoke Seminary and College, founded in 1836, started on small subscriptions, 1,800 of which amounted to $27,000.

Marietta College, founded in 1835, received her first funds of $8,000 by subscriptions and erected her second building on funds raised by subscriptions at $2 per subscriber.

---

[2] This bequest could not have been large, for in 1789, upon request, the State granted its trustees a right to raise £1,200 by lottery, the proceeds to be used to erect a building for the free school.

A very large number of these colleges began as academies. The idea of a college as an academy grown large seems to have been an accepted principle in philanthropic and State education alike.[8]

Of the 14 colleges founded between the close of the Revolution and the opening of the nineteenth century, Williams, Hampden-Sidney, Union, Hamilton, Washington and Jefferson, and Washington and Lee, all began as academies or schools of that rank, with practically no funds. The story of this period is therefore a story of simple pioneering, and that on a small scale.

HOW THE WORK WAS ACCOMPLISHED.

From the above it is clear that higher education was to be largely supported and directed by the church. The college was a definite part of the plan to propagate the Christian religion, and early in the new century the cry for an educated ministry was voiced by almost every religious publication. Response to this need in the form of church boards of education will be discussed later. It must be pointed out here, however, that between the years 1830 and 1850 the number of theological seminaries increased from 21 to 38.

This religious work in founding colleges is often denominational, as may be seen from the fifth column in Table 8. The older colleges in the East sent missionaries into the new country across the mountains to meet the " spiritual necessities of the western country,"[4] as an officer of one of the earliest colleges declares. Table 9 shows that all but 33 of the colleges of this period were established by philanthropy, 167 of the 271 being distinctly denominational projects and 71 others being religious but nonsectarian.

TABLE 9.—*Number of colleges, universities, and technical schools established during the three periods and number under the various types of control.*

Periods.	Sectarian.						Non-sectarian, but reli-gious.	Total reli-gious.	State.
	Method-ist.	Roman Catho-lic.	Bap-tist.	Pres-byte-rian.	Others.	Total.			
Colonial period, 1635–1776....	....	....	1	....	....	....	7	8	1
Early national period, 1776–1865.....................	45	31	27	27	37	167	71	238	33
Later national period, 1865–1915.....................	42	27	21	35	53	178	68	246	62

Thus the work of philanthropy through this period is to remain where it was in colonial times—in the hands of the church. There is, then, nothing specially new by way of general motive or machinery for putting that motive to work. Religion tries to meet its problems by training for religious and political leadership. It does this in the hand-to-mouth fashion to which it has long been accustomed. Williams, Amherst, Middlebury, Hamilton, and Oberlin were

---

[8] The laws of Maryland, Ch. VIII, 1782, concerning "An act for founding a college at Chestertown," says: " Whereas former legislatures of this State have, according to their best abilities, laid a considerable foundation in this good work, in sundry laws for the establishment and encouragement of county schools, for the study of Latin, Greek, writing, and the like, intending, as their future circumstances might permit, to engraft or raise on the foundation of such schools more extensive seminaries of learning by erecting one or more colleges, or places of universal study, not only in the learned languages, but in philosophy, divinity, law, physic, and other useful and ornamental arts and sciences," etc.

[4] Quarterly Register, Vol. V, p. 331.

founded very much as were Harvard, Yale, and Princeton. The problems they hoped to solve were much the same, and the methods of carrying on their work were practically the same, with the exception that early in the new century the churches began to develop boards of education through which a new type of philanthropy, aimed directly at the preparation of a trained ministry, was administered.

Further detailed study of the development of philanthropy in the older foundations, in typical foundations of this period, and of church boards of education should bring to light any new ideas or methods of work which the philanthropy of this period has to offer.

PHILANTHROPY IN THE OLDER COLLEGES.

1. A PERIOD OF SMALL GIFTS, SMALL INCOME, AND SMALL ENDOWMENT.

To follow out the developments which took place in the older foundations we have to refer again to Tables 2, 3, 4, 5, and 6, where the data discussed in chapter 3 are carried forward.

These colleges passed through the stormy period of the Revolution, in which they all suffered more or less. Yet they survived, and an examination of the total columns in these tables seems to indicate that the spirit of philanthropy was kept alive through it all. The total gifts to Harvard during the years 1771–1775 were relatively large, though they dropped during the decade following. Yale and Princeton, on the other hand, received but little by way of gifts during this period, but came well up to their average during the decade following, while King's College appears not to have been affected seriously.

Aside from a few large gifts just before the Civil War, this was a period of small gifts for these old colleges. Harvard depended upon small subscriptions to erect Divinity Hall in 1826, to establish a professorship of natural history in 1805, and a professorship of geology in 1820. More than three-fourths of Yale's endowment fund of $100,000 was raised in 1831 and 1832 by Wyllis Warner in a similar way.[5]

It was also a time when permanent endowments were small, and when the colleges were often struggling with heavy deficits. Yale's income from invested funds in 1831 amounted to but $2,300, while the income from tuition was too small to cover the necessary expenditures of $15,474.[6] In appealing to the legislature for aid in 1822, Yale declared her debt to be $11,000, with permanent productive funds of but $20,000. In 1825 Harvard's expenditures exceeded her income by more than $4,000, while as late as 1840 her productive funds amounted to only about $156,126.[7] Rhode Island College changed her name to Brown University in 1804 for a gift of $5,000.

An examination of the total columns in these four tables shows that it was not only a period of small gifts but also one of small total income. With the funds that were at the disposal of Yale in 1800, it is not surprising that the ambition of the college to become a university could be satisfied with the establishment of schools of law, medicine, and theology in terms of a single professorship for each of those fields.

---

[5] Baldwin, reissue of "Annals of Yale," appendix, presents list of subscribers.

[6] Steiner, B. C. Hist. of Educ. in Conn., p. 152, Washington, D. C., 1893.

[7] Quincy, "History of Harvard College," II, 360, makes the former of these statements on authority of the treasurer's report of that year. The second is from the treasurer's report of 1840, ibid., appendix No. LX.

2. EXPANSION OF THE COLLEGE AND INCREASE OF CONDITIONAL GIFTS.

Our concern here is not with the mere size of the gift, however, but particularly with the conditions upon which the gift is received. As a college expands from one to many buildings, from a classical to a scientific program, from one to many instructors—in other words, from a traditional college to a university—its needs tend to become more and more diverse, and so, specific, as opposed to general. The donor who in the old day saw only the college now sees laboratories, various kinds of professorships, buildings, libraries, departments of this and that, etc., and if not consulted about his gift, is less likely to give to the "college," since the college has now become a vague and indefinite thing.

Amid such developments we should expect gifts to be made less frequently to the general funds of the institution, and more often to a single specified part of it. An examination of columns four and five of our tables shows that this was roughly the tendency in all cases. The per cent given to "general fund," with some exceptions, gradually grows smaller and the per cent to "specified purposes" larger.

The question arises as to whether the new departures were more often initiated by the president or board of trustees or by some donor who conceived the idea and proposed its adoption by offering to endow it. This can not be answered fully for the reason that all the facts concerning the naming of conditions upon which a gift is offered can not now be obtained. It appears that most of the gifts of this period were conditional. While it is true that the new professorships, by way of which new departments and schools were usually opened up, are named in memory of some special donor,[8] yet we can not be sure that growth in these terms was not largely directed by the college.

3. HOW THE GIFTS WERE CONDITIONED.

A second question of interest about a gift is whether it is to be available for immediate use or to become a part of the productive funds of the college. During colonial times, as was pointed out above, gifts were most generally for immediate use. That is slightly less true for this period, as may be seen from a study of columns six and seven of the table. It is decidedly less true for Harvard, whose "permanent endowment" funds show a steady growth all through the period.

A further study of these tables will show the conditions under which the early narrow streams of beneficence flowing into these colleges gradually widened during these 90 years. The library column would be enlarged if all of the gifts of books could have been included. It appears that the library received proportionately less at Yale through this period than it had been receiving, that no money gifts went to the libraries at Columbia and at Princeton, while at Harvard such gifts increased slightly and became more constant.

The first professorship ever founded in this country was that of divinity at Harvard, endowed by Thomas Hollis in 1721. There were five others founded in Harvard, Yale, and Princeton during the colonial period, after which almost a constant stream of gifts at Harvard and Princeton are for this purpose. At Yale no gifts for this purpose are recorded from 1760 to 1820. After this date, however, there is a fairly regular and substantial tendency to endow instruction. Columbia has had much less of this kind of assistance, there having been but one such large gift ($20,000 in 1843) previous to the year 1896. The de-

---

[8] Of the 35 professorships and lectureships established at Harvard by 1865, 26 were named for some benefactor of the college.

velopments in this particular line of giving coincide roughly with the period of expansion of the little traditional college into a university.

Reference to the " pious and indigent students " column in these tables shows that at Harvard the gifts to this cause are irregular and relatively less than in the earlier years; at Princeton they become more regular and relatively larger. At Yale, where no such gifts appear before 1821, the response is irregular and slight. At Columbia practically no gifts are for the " poor and pious."

Assistance to students direct comes through another channel (see scholarship and fellowship columns of the tables), in which poverty and piety play no part. It has long been the custom to give money to pay the tuition of the brightest student, as judged by competitive examination, and from our tables this continues to be supported. Before 1835 Harvard and Princeton show much more interest in the poor and pious than in this group. Yale tends to favor the competitive scholarship idea, and at Columbia, where the poor and pious receive little or no attention, a large and constant proportion of gifts go to scholarships and fellowships.

One other way of helping the student directly is by use of prizes. Account was kept of such gifts, but they proved to be irregular in all cases and of no great consequence, so they do not appear in the tables. By adding together the two items " scholarships " and " pious and indigent students " in the tables we see that there is much educational philanthrophy which chooses to go directly to the student rather than indirectly through provision of instructors, library, laboratory, buildings, etc. It is not the large educational enterprise in which such donors are interested ; it is an individual, and philanthropy is with them a personal matter, that is, true charity.

4. LARGE GIFTS OF THE PERIOD.

There were a few large gifts received during this period. Leaving out the funds raised by subscription, the important gifts to three of the old colonial colleges during this period are recorded in Table 10, which shows their form, date, amount, and purpose.

TABLE 10.—*Amounts and conditions of the large gifts to Harvard, Yale, and Columbia from 1776 to 1865.*

College.	Date.	Form of donation.	Amount.	Conditions controlling gift.
Harvard......	1814	Gift........	$20,000	To found professorship of Greek.
Harvard......	1816	Bequest...	20,000	To found professorship of French, Spanish, and literature.
Harvard......	1845	...do.......	100,000	Unrestricted (to advance virtue, science, and literature.)
Harvard......	1848	...do.......	50,000	Education of young men of rare powers.
Harvard......	1854	...do.......	50,000	To erect a chapel.
Yale..........	1825	Gift.......	25,000	"On specified conditions."
Yale..........	1860	...do.......	50,000	To endow Sheffield Scientific School.
Yale..........	1863	...do.......	40,000	To endow professorship of divinity.
Yale..........	1863	...do.......	50,000	To endow professorship of Sanscrit.
Yale..........	1864	...do.......	175,000	Building for art school.
Yale..........	1864–1867	...do.......	60,000	Building for a dormitory.
Yale..........	1865	...do.......	30,000	For a college chapel.
Columbia.....	1843	Bequest...	20,000	To endow a professorship.

It would certainly be difficult to question the conditions placed upon these gifts. There are 13 in all, 5 for the founding of professorships, 4 for buildings, 1 for endowment of a scientific school. 1 for scholarships, 1 " on specified conditions " which are not known, and 1 unrestricted.

These gifts represent departures but not wide departures from the ordinary college. The French influence is seen in the establishment of a French and Spanish professorship, the first of its kind in this country.[9] The influence of the scientific movement also is shown by the professorships of natural history and mineralogy and geology which were established in 1805 and 1820.

It is noteworthy that but one of these gifts is to go to the student direct. The conditions of the gift provide that young men of rare powers in any department of knowledge may be helped, not only after they enter Harvard but even before, wherever they may be found.

Thus it appears that the large gifts of this period provided only for normal expansion of the colleges, and probably did not anticipate, except in point of time, the growth that would have come had these colleges been provided with unconditional instead of conditional gifts.

Reference to the dates will show how few were the gifts of this size previous to the middle of the nineteenth century. As to form, those to Harvard and Columbia are mostly by bequest, while those to Yale are by gift direct.

5. FORM OF THE GIFTS.

Turning again to the last two columns of Tables 3 to 6 for a study of the form of the benefactions, we find that at Harvard there is a slight increase in the " bequests " column during this period, but that at Yale, Princeton, and Columbia the burden of the income is by direct gift.

In these tables, then, which are doubtless typical for all the older colleges, the developments show that the total gifts to the colleges do not increase much before the second quarter of the new century. By that time income from the State had grown very irregular or stopped entirely. There was a tendency to change from giving " to the college " to giving to some special feature of the college. Permanent endowment received more attention than before and there was a falling off of interest in the " pious and indigent," except at Princeton. There was an increased interest in scholarships and fellowships and a rapidly growing interest in professorships; and gifts rather than bequests, Harvard excepted, remained the favorite form of benefactions.

PHILANTHROPY IN THE COLLEGES FOUNDED LATER.

As shown already, the increase in the number of colleges kept pace with the development of the country, the church continuing as chief sponsor for the promotion of higher education. A large percentage of the colleges were definitely denominational projects, aimed at the development of a trained ministry and the spread of religious and classical knowledge among laymen. They were often the outgrowth of academies, many of which were started on very small funds obtained by subscription (as Middlebury College from an academy with funds amounting to $4,000).

Being in many cases the offspring of the older colleges, developed largely by and for the people of the East who had moved westward, promoted by the same ministry as that which had founded and nourished the colonial colleges,[10]

---

[9] Bush, ibid., p. 85, quotes this statement from President Eliot.

[10] According to tenth annual report of directors of the American College and Education Society a substantial stream of gifts was constantly flowing from eastern donors to the struggling young colleges of the West. The following figures show the amounts of

under very similar frontier and financial conditions we expect the colleges, as well as the nature and methods of their support and control, to resemble those of the older colleges in the East. In general, in fact one could almost say in detail, this resemblance did exist. Amherst College is typical for the period. In Table 11 is shown a distribution of its gifts from its origin in 1821 to 1890. The college originated as Amherst Academy, a subscription fund for which was started in 1812. The school opened in 1814 and by 1818 was beginning the collection of funds for the future college. Amherst is one of the nine New England colleges founded during this period and began its career both as an academy and as a college on money collected by subscription. Its first funds, $51,404, were collected to found a "Charity Institution," and the great care with which the conditions controlling the administration of this fund are set forth [11] impresses one with the missionary zeal of the founders. Article three of this document provides that five-sixths of the interest of the fund shall be forever appropriated to the classical education in the institution of indigent pious young men for the ministry, and the other sixth shall be added to the principal for its perpetual increase, while the principal shall be secured intact and perpetually augmenting.[12] Here, in the conditions controlling this foundation gift, is evidence of the religious aim of the college and of its acceptance of the policy of subsidizing young men who qualify as "indigent, pious, and desirous of entering the ministry." While not the same in detail, this sounds much like the beginning of a colonial college.

For a number of years Amherst's history has much to say about poverty, but a comparison of the total benefactions to Amherst in her early years with those for Harvard, Princeton, and Yale in Tables 3, 4, and 5 shows that Amherst fared somewhat better in her infancy than did these older colleges, even allowing for differences in money values. In the face of her fairly real competition for funds with Harvard, Yale, and Williams, on the average her income compares favorably with that of Princeton during the years 1821–1830, and then rapidly surpasses Princeton, Harvard, and Yale for a number of years.

---

these gifts by years from 1844 to 1884. This is mostly the work of the Congregational Church. If the many other church societies did as well, then this represents an important source of support for western colleges.

1844	$15,588	1854	$11,250	1865	$14,710	1875	$62,375
1845	9,500	1855	15,077	1866	23,588	1876	38,691
1846	14,000	1856	18,887	1867	35,246	1877	34,516
1847	12,555	1857	12,131	1868	51,319	1878	42,221
1848	10,000	1858	8,428	1869	19,964	1879	37,994
1849	34,300	1859	10,159	1870	65,695	1880	38,983
1850	41,500	1860	18,291	1871	72,425	1881	229,851
1851	20,500	1861–62	10,298	1872	51,022	1882	64,228
1852	19,000	1863	14,689	1873	73,881	1883	135,344
1853	13,496	1864	56,320	1874	52,979	1884	88,137

These amounts were contributed to the following institutions:

Western Reserve College, Ohio.
Marietta College, Ohio.
Lane Theological Seminary, Ohio.
Wittenberg College, Ohio.
Heidelberg College, Ohio.
Oberlin College, Ohio.
Wilberforce University, Ohio.
Illinois College, Illinois.
Knox College, Illinois.
Wabash College, Indiana.
Beloit College, Wisconsin.
Ripon College, Wisconsin.
Washburn College, Kansas.

Iowa College, Iowa.
Yellow Springs College, Iowa.
German Evangelical College, Missouri.
Webster College, Missouri.
Thayer College, Missouri.
Drury College, Missouri.
Pacific University, Oregon.
College of St. Paul, Minnesota.
Carleton College, Minnesota.
College of California, California.
Pacific Theological Seminary, California.
Olivet College, Michigan.
Berea College, Kentucky.

[11] See W. S. Tyler, "A History of Amherst College," p. 7 ff., for a full statement of the 14 articles controlling the fund.

[12] The report of the treasurer of Amherst College for 1912 shows this fund to be $95,098.50.

TABLE 11.—*Donations and grants to Amherst College, 1821–1890—Distribution of gifts by individuals.*[1]

Dates.	Grants by States.	Gifts by individuals.	Per cent of total gifts by individuals for—										Per cent in form of—		Collected by subscription.
			General fund.	Specified purpose.	Present use.	Permanent endowment.	Scholarships and fellowships.	Professorships.	Pious and indigent students.	Library.	Prize.	Building and plant.	Gift.	Bequest.	
1819 [2]	....	[2] $51,404	......	100	.....	100	....	.....	100	....	.....	.....	100	.....	100
1821–1830	....	34,000	......	100	100	....	....	....	....	....	.....	100	88	12	88
1831–1839	....	54,000	99.0	1	100	....	....	....	6.5	1.5	.....	....	100	.....	99
1840–1845	....	100,000	......	36	64	36	....	15	....	....	.....	....	89	11	100
1845–1854	$25,000	108,000	......	100	31	69	....	57	....	14	.....	....	100	.....	13
1855–1860	....	67,692	......	64	96	4	4	....	....	3	.....	....	70	30	16
1861–1865	27,500	260,000	1.5	98.5	77	23	....	23	....	3	1	74	98.5	1.5	....
1866–1870	....	156,976	......	100	100	....	....	....	....	4	.....	....	4	96	....
1871–1875	....	257,000	......	100	33	67	52	9	....	....	5	....	100	.....	....
1876–1890	....	881,895	1.7	83	41	59	7	22	....	8	0.5	11	78	22	4

[1] Sources from which these data were taken: W. S. Tyler, "A History of Amherst College;" Geo. Gary Bush, Hist. of Higher Educa. in Mass.
[2] Known as the charity fund. One-sixth of income to be added to principal annually. In his 1912 report the college treasurer shows this fund to be $95,098.50.

To show how completely acceptable this new college was to the people, however narrow and local its constituency, we need only to look at the attendance and size of the teaching staff from the beginning to 1894. While there was a serious drop in attendance about 1840 to 1850, there was a steady rise. The tuition charges for these years were as follows:

1821–1833	$30–$33	1847–1855	$30	1871–1875	$90
1833–1834	27	1855–1864	36	1875–1886	100
1836–1847	33	1864–1868	45	1886	100
1834–1836	30	1868–1871	75		

It is evident that the income from tuition was not great, and since in the earlier years of the college nothing was received from the State, practically the whole burden was carried by philanthropy. How this was done is of some interest.

Table 11 gives a fair description, one striking feature of which is the final column, which shows what per cent of all gifts were obtained by the subscription method. Aside from this the table offers little that is different from what we have seen in the older colleges for this period. Most of the gifts have been conditional, but when we look at the following columns in the table and see that professorships, library, and buildings have fared so well, it appears that the conditions placed upon the gifts were expressions of real needs. In the early years, as in the older colleges, most of the gifts were available for immediate use, with a slight tendency toward permanent endowments later.

Aside from the charity subscription at the beginning, which is a scholarship fund for ministerial students, no scholarships were founded till 1857, when about 50 were established. But little money for prizes was received during this period; so that the amount of gifts direct to students, aside from the foundation subscription fund, is small in comparison with that given to the library or for professorships or for buildings.

Professorships fared about as well as they did in the older colleges during these same years, while indigence is not subsidized after the initial gift. As at Yale, Princeton, and Columbia, most of the benefactions are by gift rather than by bequest.

THEOLOGICAL EDUCATION OF THIS PERIOD.

In 1912–13 there were 179 theological schools reporting to the United States Commissioner of Education, 70 of which were founded during this period. These schools show permanent endowment funds of nearly $40,000,000, and since they are all the work of philanthropy and have from the start constituted a prominent feature of higher education in this country some consideration of the methods of philanthropy in their development is pertinent to this study.

The first separately organized school of this type founded in the United States was the Andover Theological Seminary, established in 1808. The lengthy creed of this school was carefully prepared by the two wings of Calvinists and has been publicly read and subscribed to by each professor on his inauguration and before the trustees every fifth year since the foundation.[13] This is how strictly denominational the school has been.

In 1913 the school reported a plant worth $300,000 and nearly three-quarters of a million dollars in permanent endowment funds.[14] It received initial gifts of buildings and $60,000, and before the close of this period possessed five endowed professorships.

TABLE 12.—*Gifts to permanent funds of Andover Theological Seminary, 1807 to 1890.*[1]

Dates.	Total amount.	General fund.	Professorships.	Library.	Scholarships.
1807–1810	$75,000	$30,000	$45,000		
1811–1815	79,000		79,000		
1816–1820	25,000		25,000		
1831–1835	15,000		15,000		
1841–1845	80,000	80,000			
1856–1860	53,000		25,000		
1866–1870	119,000		[2] 64,000	$25,000	
1871–1875	95,000		43,000		
1876–1880	240,000		50,000	20,000	
1881–1885	14,000				
1886–1890	315,000			28,000	$97,000

[1] Data for this table obtained from Geo. Gary Bush's Hist. of Higher Ed. in Mass., 1891.
[2] Of this amount, $10,000 was for the establishment of a lectureship.

Table 12 shows the distribution of the permanent funds of the institution. From this table it will be seen that no great part of its gifts for permanent endowment have gone to the general fund, that nothing has gone to scholarships or to indigent and pious students or to prizes, but that many gifts have gone to endow professorships. Only $28,000 of these amounts seems to have been received by way of small subscriptions.

The Bangor Theological Seminary was established in 1814 by the Society for Promoting Theological Education. This was one of the earliest education societies in America. Its purpose was—

raising a fund to assist those well-disposed young men that are desirous of entering in the work of the gospel ministry, but by deficiency of pecuniary resources are unable to prosecute a course of regular studies necessary to qualify them for a station so important and useful.[15] "The Maine Charity School," as it was then called, was established for the purpose of promoting religion, morality, etc. Only native-born citizens could ever become trustees.

[13] Bush, p. 240.
[14] Rep. U. S. Com. of Edu., 1913, p. 325.
[15] Hall: Higher Educ. in Maine, p. 35.

In the early days the school had no endowment and marks its first important gift as $300. In 1835 a $100,000 endowment fund was started, but because of the financial crisis of that time only about one-third of this amount was raised. Another effort was made in 1849, when $34,000 was raised for the endowment of two professorships. Since that date the school has prospered. In 1913 a permanent endowment of $310,000 was reported.

These are but samples to show how philanthropy, entirely unaided by the State, took care of education for this particular profession.

OTHER LINES OF PROFESSIONAL TRAINING.

What philanthrophy has not done is of some interest here, since we are concerned with its relation to the development of all higher education.

Theology has been kept strictly apart from politics in this country, and aside from a few early gifts from the State, this profession has been built up entirely by philanthrophy. Its institutional growth was in the beginning in connection with colleges of liberal training, but toward the close of the eighteenth century began to develop as separate schools. This was partly in fear of the rather unorthodox trend in the colleges and partly in order to better the instruction, since the demand for a better-trained ministry appears to have been strong. Denominationalism was also a factor in the case of churches which had not established colleges of their own.

While higher education for the ministry has been handled entirely by philanthropy, this has not been true of either law or medicine. A few professorships of law [16] and physic were established in the universities before the end of the colonial period, but appear to have been too academic and indirect to satisfy the rather utilitarian motives of these two professions. In the beginning, in fact all through this period, and even later, a few busy doctors taught medicine, and law was learned almost wholly by apprenticeship despite the rapidly increasing importance of the legal profession after the Revolution.[17]

EDUCATION OF WOMEN.

Another important educational movement in the history of higher education which originates during this period, and furnishes new motives to philanthropy, is that of colleges for women. The movement takes its rise along with Jacksonian democracy, antislavery agitation, the great westward movement, and early women's rights agitation, and very quickly takes permanent form in the hands of philanthropy, first through the pioneer work of Mrs. Emma Willard in the founding of the Troy Female Seminary in 1820 and the later work of Miss Mary Lyon in connection with the founding of Mount Holyoke Seminary and College in 1836.

After an interesting educational career, Mrs. Willard opened the Troy Female Seminary in 1821. An initial fund of $4,000 was raised by the city of Troy by taxation and promptly supplemented by gifts. According to the curriculum offered,[18] it is fair to look upon this as a genuine and successful attempt at higher education for women, even though the school later passed out of existence.

In every sense this was a philanthropic enterprise. It succeeded as such for some 70 years, during which time it wielded a very wide influence and

[16] Professorships of law were established at William and Mary in 1799; at the University of Pennsylvania in 1790; at Columbia in 1793; at Yale in 1801; at Dartmouth in 1808; and at Harvard in 1815.

[17] See Professional Distribution of College and University Graduates, by Bailey B. Burritt, U. S. Bu. of Ed. Bul., 1912, No. 19.

[18] See U. S. Com. of Ed. Rep., 1895–96, Vol. I, pp. 240–257.

stood as one of the important foundation stones which Mrs. Willard laid for the higher education of women in this country.

Miss Lyon, like Mrs. Willard, proceeded on the assumption that it was quite as important to enlist the interest and sympathy of the great mass of people as it was to secure funds. She planned, therefore, to raise $30,000 by small subscriptions to start Mount Holyoke Seminary and College. When one reads that one of the record books of subscriptions contained the names of more than 1,800 subscribers from 90 places, promising a total of $27,000, in sums varying from 6 cents to $1,000,[19] and then reads that it was Miss Lyon's wish to " put within the reach of students of moderate means such opportunities that none can find better * * * a permanent institution consecrated to the work of training young women to the greatest usefulness," and one " designed to be furnished with every advantage that the state of education in this country will allow,[20] he realizes that, while philanthropy is not finding new methods, it is finding a new motive in an institution exclusively for the higher education of women.

As is well known, the new idea met with opposition but, as usual, it was finally proved that philanthropy can be depended upon to meet any important social need as soon as that need differentiates itself from mere vague unrest.

This movement for the education of women was less than 30 years old when the founder of Vassar College laid down funds amounting to nearly $800,000 for a similar institution, so much in demand as to attract nearly 350 students in its first year. Thus in a short time philanthropy's experiment had succeeded far beyond expectations.

PHILANTHROPY AND THE MANUAL-LABOR COLLEGES.

The manual-labor movement in American secondary and higher education came to this country from Europe, where for nearly the first half of the nineteenth century Fellenberg and his successors experimented with the idea of combining remunerative work with school training. Students from many countries visited the Fellenberg institution, and the movement spread rapidly, the labor features finding a fertile field in both colleges and secondary schools in this country. In Connecticut as early as 1819 such a school was established, and in 1831 the manual labor society for promoting manual labor in literary institutions was organized. The secretary of this society made an extended tour of the West and Southwest, visiting the manual labor schools, but seems to have left no statistical evidence of his study.

Where the idea was introduced here the labor feature was used as an appeal to the philanthropist for support and to the parent to send his son to college, where, as a Wesleyan University resolution of August 27, 1833, says, " the physical as well as the intellectual and moral education will be attended to."

It is only necessary to state that this idea took form in Maine Wesleyan Seminary in 1825, in Andover Theological Seminary in 1826, in Colby College in 1827, in Western Reserve University in 1830, in Wesleyan University in 1833, in Hartford Theological Seminary in 1834, and in Oberlin from its origin in 1833, to show something of the type of colleges which introduced it and the extent of its adoption. It was an expression of a new social as well as educa-

---

[19] Mount Holyoke Seminary and College, by Mrs. Sarah D. (Locke) Stowe, U. S. Bu. of Ed. Circ. No. 6, 1891, Ch. XXII.

[20] " Mount Holyoke College—the Seventy-fifth Anniversary," p. 13.

tional philosophy, and seems to have made its appeal for benefactions from the social, moral, religious, educational, and economic points of view.

A more intimate study of the benefactions to Oberlin, a college founded after the movement had become popular and one which fairly hewed its way into the world on the manual-labor basis, should give us a fair picture of this type of educational philanthropy.

Mr. Leonard,[21] quoting from Oberlin's first annual report, 1834, says: "The manual labor department is indispensable to complete education" and, "in a word, it meets the wants of a man as a compound being and prevents common and amazing waste of money, time, health, and life." He then goes on to explain the nature and extent of the department and how well it is working. In 1837 "nearly all the young ladies and a majority of the young gentlemen have paid their board by manual labor." This report adds that while the school's funds were as they found them at that time, no pledge could be made that labor would be furnished. From then on the failure of the scheme was only a matter of time, and in 1849 the trustees realized that it was not paying and that some legal means of ending the experiment must be found.

It was at this point that the "dead hand" appeared. The 500 acres of land had been donated to a *manual labor school.* In 1852 legal authority was found for leasing the ground, the lessee covenanting "yearly, during said term, to employ students of said college in some department of manual labor (when applied for) and pay them for their labor the current market price, to an amount each year of at least $2 for each acre of land hereby demised." [22] Further on in the lease it is agreed that in case any part of the lease is adjudged to be beyond the powers of the Oberlin trustees, the lease becomes void. The expression "manual labor" disappeared from the catalogue after 1867–68, and in place of it reference is made to "facilities for self-support."

Thus within 2 years from the beginning the college had failed to meet the full demand for labor, and within 20 years the labor scheme had disappeared in failure. During these 20 years, however, Oberlin had become a fairly well-established college, though these had been years of extreme poverty with much debt.

The school's first real funds, some $15,000, were received during the first year, largely upon solicitation in payment for scholarships.[23] The business side of the undertaking soon used this money, and the college went begging to New York, where it received a guarantee for full endowment of eight professorships. An unalterable condition of this gift, which was never paid, was that Negroes should be given equal privilege with white students in the school.

In this gift we have an illustration of how the policy of a college respecting a very important social and political issue was to be absolutely settled by philanthropy, and settled contrary to the wishes of nearly half the trustees of the college. A second effect of this intended gift was the abolition of all tuition charges, a move which cost the college dearly.

Within a few years the college was some $40,000 in debt. In 1837 an effort to raise a $100,000 endowment realized only about $6,000.[24] Finally, in 1839,

---

[21] The Story of Oberlin, by Delavan L. Leonard, p. 224 ff.

[22] Leonard, ibid., p. 228.

[23] These perpetual scholarships cost $150 each and paid no tuition, merely giving the holder the privilege of entering the school and using the labor appliances to earn his way. They were thus a further pledge that the labor feature would be perpetuated.

[24] Commons: Hist. of Higher Educ. in Ohio.

agents were sent to England to make an appeal for help with which to pay the debts of the college.[25] This brought $30,000 and valuable collections of books, and deserves notice here because the agents carried with them to England letters from antislavery leaders in America through which they presented their case to antislavery sympathizers in England. This and the idea of education for women are said to have made special appeal to the Society of Friends in England.[26]

Little aside from a gift of 20,000 acres of land was received during the next decade, but in 1850 an attempt at endowment was made, and by 1852 almost $95,000 was raised and invested. This, however, was another sale of scholarships, which this time secured free tuition for one student perpetually for $100, 18 years for $50, and 6 years for $25. This was merely paying tuition in advance, but a little figuring will show that it must be counted an absurdly low tuition. The interest on $100 could not possibly pay the cost of educating a student. Thus the college increased its business,[27] but on an unsound economic basis, which broke down with the high cost of living in the sixties.

This is a fair picture of the relation of philanthropy to the manual labor college movement. There is little to distinguish it from the philanthropy in the old colleges where the manual labor idea was never adopted. It is just more evidence that philanthropy in education has been governed by the conditions of the times rather than by any wise educational philosophy. The manual labor college was but an incident in our great westward expansion. Such cure-all schemes in education were essential to the times. Hartford Theological Seminary carefully avoided the " incubus " of any permanent fund for the first few years, but when her subscribers fell off and lost their zeal for giving, an $11,000 bequest was gladly accepted as permanent endowment.

Kenyon College sent out an appeal, " The Star in the West, or Kenyon College in the Year of Our Lord 1828," calling upon the reader to send $1 to the struggling school. " Kenyon College Circles " were formed in numerous towns where women met and sewed for the college, and more than $25,000 was sent in as the result of this appeal.

On the whole it is wiser to say that the manual labor movement was useful because it expressed an essential element in the civilization of that time than to say that it was useless because it was educationally and economically impossible.

PHILANTHROPHY THROUGH EDUCATION SOCIETIES.

Another channel through which philanthropy has played a part in American higher education is that of religious education societies. These societies began to organize early in the nineteenth century in response to the demand for trained missionaries and ministers. Statistics published in early numbers of the American Quarterly Register show that churches were fully conscious of this need.

Aside from several small local societies, the American Education Society[28] was the initial undertaking in this field, its original constitution being dated August

---

[25] Fairchild : Oberlin, the Colony and the College, p. 208.

[26] Ibid., p. 209.

[27] This immediately increased the number of students from 570 to 1,020.

[28] In 1874 the American Education Society and the Society for the Promotion of Collegiate and Theological Education in the West were united under the name American College and Education Society. See their annual reports for 1874.

29, 1815.[29] The aim of this society is made clear by the following statement from its original constitution:

Taking into serious consideration the deplorable condition of the inhabitants of these United States, the greater part of whom are either destitute of competent religious instruction or exposed to the errors and enthusiasm of unlearned men, we * * * do hereby, * * * form ourselves into a society for the benevolent purpose of aiding, and of exciting others to aid, indigent young men of talents and hopeful piety in acquiring a learned and competent education for the Gospel Ministry.

This outlines a definite piece of work to be done, proposes philanthropy as a means, and *indigent young men of talents and hopeful of piety* as the agency for doing it.

Further on in the constitution it is proposed to raise funds by subscription, and it is stated that "a permanent fund, of which five-sixths part of the interest only may be expended, shall be formed of bequests, legacies, donations, grants, and subscriptions," and further, that agents shall be appointed to solicit—

by exciting churches and congregations to make annual collections for this purpose; and by establishing auxiliary societies in towns, counties, and distant regions, together with Cent Societies, * * * by personal and persevering addresses to rich individuals of both sexes, * * * and by respectful applications to legislative bodies and other classes of men; by establishing active and extensive correspondences, etc.

All appropriations of funds are to be made by the trustees, who will also examine and select the candidates for the charity. All recipients of the charity who do not enter the ministry must refund the money received. The final article declares that " This Constitution, but not its object, may be altered and amended."

The plans by which aid was granted have been changed from time to time,[30] but since 1842 the money has been given as a gratuity.

The bases for eligibility of applicants for assistance are stated in general terms only. Up to 1841 the applicant must have had 6 months of classical studies. During 1841 this was increased to 12 months, and in 1842 to college entrance requirements, with the exception of third-year academy students in some cases. This exception was later abolished.

Such has been the general aim and plans of work of one of the oldest of these societies in America. To describe the workings of the other societies of this type would be practically to repeat the above. The Presbyterian Education Society was founded in 1819, became a branch of the American Education Society in 1827 [31] and operated as such until the break in the Presbyterian Church, which took place toward the close of the period under discussion. The society for educating pious young men for the ministry of the Protestant Episcopal Church was organized in 1818 and within a decade had 28 auxiliary societies

---

[29] A copy of this constitution is printed in full in Appendix A of the annual report of the society for 1839.

Whether this idea of organizing education societies for the training of ministers was borrowed from England is not known, but such a society existed in England as early as 1648. The American Quarterly Register, vol. 3, pp. 145–152, published a tract showing "a model for the maintaining of students of choice abilities at the university, and principally in order to the ministry," followed by the names of trustees, among which were Matthew Poole, Richard Baxter, Wm. Bates, and others. In Chapter IV of the model we read: " That the scholars to be chosen be of godly life, or at the least, hopeful for godliness, of eminent parts, of an ingenious disposition, and such as are poor, or have not a sufficient maintenance any other way." This society had 44 students at Oxford and Cambridge at this time.

[30] See An. Rep. for 1839, p. 71 ff; also Barnard's Amer. J. of Educ., vol. 14, p. 373 ff.

[31] An. Rep. Amer. Ed. Soc., 1839.

operating under its supervision.[82] The Massachusetts Baptist Education Society, later the board of education of the Northern Baptist Church, starting in 1814; the board of education of the Reformed Dutch Church, starting in 1828; the board of education of the Methodist Episcopal Church, starting in 1864; and the Society for the Promotion of Collegiate and Theological Education in the West are the principal organizations of this type. Each of these had numerous branch societies, and all supported students in part or in full by loans.

The development of branch or auxiliary societies in connection with the American Education Society is a fair sample of their methods. Between 1815 and 1838 there were organized 63 branch societies east of the Mississippi River and north of the southern boundary of Tennessee; 41 of these were founded between 1829 and 1834.[83]

Although the chief method of work was by direct gift or loan to the student, in some cases professorships were established, salaries were paid, and buildings erected. The gifts or loans to students were often no more than $40 per year.

In 1829 to 1831 there were 18 to 22 theological seminaries in operation in the United States. Table 13 shows the number of students attending these schools and the number receiving aid from some education society.[84]

From this it appears that from one-fourth to one-sixth of the theological students in the United States at this time were beneficiaries of these organizations.

Table 15 sets forth for each fifth year, which may be taken as representative of the other years, the financial history of three of these societies, along with the numbers of beneficiaries they have had under their care during this period.

Table 14 shows what a large part of the student body at Amherst College was receiving assistance from the American Education Society.

TABLE 13.—*Number of students in theological seminaries and number receiving aid from religious education societies.*

Dates.	Students in seminaries.	Receiving aid.
1829	599	151
1830	639	143
1831	709	115

TABLE 14.—*Number of students attending Amherst College, 1845–1854, and number and per cent of these receiving aid from the American Educational Society.*[a]

Dates.	Total students attending.	Receiving aid from American Education Society.	
		Number.	Per cent.
1845	118	27	22.8
1846	120	28	23.3
1847	150	26	17.3
1848	166	45	27.1
1849	176	42	23.8
1850	182	57	31.3
1851	190	56	29.0
1852	195	46	23.5
1853	211	40	19.0
1854	237	58	24.5

a Data for this table taken from Edward H. Hitchcock's Reminiscences of Amherst College.

[82] Amer. Quar. Register, Jan., 1829, p. 190.

[83] From An. Rep. Am. Educ. Soc. for 1839, pp. 88–90.

[84] Data taken from Am. Quar. Register, vol. 1, p. 220; vol. 2, p. 247; vol. 3, p. 303.

TABLE 15.—*Showing for each fifth year the annual receipts and the number of students aided by three church or religious educational societies.*[1]

Date.	American Educ. Society.		Northern Baptist Educ. Society.		Presbyterian Educ. Society.	
	Amount received.	Number aided.	Amount received.	Number aided.	Amount received.	Number aided.
1817	$5,714	138	$604	11		
1822	13,108	195	2,049	9	$4,457	90
1827	33,092	300	2,245	19	11,860	230
1832	41,927	807	5,340	33	13,761	270
1837	65,574	1,125			37,038	562
1842	32,352	615			26,628	300
1847	32,831	389			39,545	403
1852	15,565	413			45,396	372
1857	28,732	332			48,632	383
1862	16,559	324			43,244	375
1865	23,386	200			51,308	254

[1] Compiled from the volumes of the American Quarterly Register and from the annual reports of the societies.

One of these societies, the Society for the Promotion of Collegiate and Theological Education in the West, had a slightly different purpose. It was organized in 1844, and operated as a separate society down to 1874, at which time it joined with the American Education Society. Its purpose as set forth in its charter [35] was to assist struggling young colleges in the West with funds collected in eastern churches.[36] It was concerned with general as well as with theological training, and limited its aid not only to western colleges but only to such of these as showed promise. There is evidence that this society had influence in the development of higher standards in western colleges.[37]

TABLE 16.—*Financial account of the Society for the Promotion of Collegiate and Theological Education in the West.*

Years.	Receipts.	Grants.	Colleges aided.	Years.	Receipts.	Grants.	Colleges aided.
1844	$17,004	$15,588	5	1859	$15,185	$10,156	10
1845	11,661	8,704	5	1860	22,528	17,793	11
1846	15,730	13,194		1863	18,643	14,689	7
1847	14,113	14,324	7	1864	60,270	56,320	6
1848	12,339		7	1865	20,430	14,710	7
1849	16,737		7	1866	26,913	23,588	4
1850	17,623		6	1867	38,538	33,246	5
1851	16,962		6	1868	58,426	51,319	6
1852	20,617		7	1869	27,803	19,964	9
1853	20,931	12,296	11	1870	72,289	65,695	6
1854	17,803	9,669	11	1871	74,742	72,425	7
1855	19,021	6,978	4	1872	62,475	51,022	7
1856	24,687	18,889	16	1873	76,505	73,881	7
1857	18,007	11,692	8	1874	57,760	52,979	9
1858	14,103	8,418	12				

Table 16, showing the work done by the society, will bear close study. The society gave aid " to the college," not to individual students, and did this in a way to keep down useless undertakings and to stimulate useful ones.

If we compare the income of these societies with that of colleges reported in Tables 2, 3, 4, 5, 10, 11, and 12, we will see that in these early years the work of these societies is by no means a mere incident in the educational machinery.

[35] See the society's first annual report, 1844.

[36] " It is an eastern society. Not a western vote affects the decisions of the board." Fifth an. rep., 1848, p. 7.

[37] See annual report for 1845, p. 12.

From 1821 to 1825 Yale received by gift approximately $16,000 annually; Princeton less than $2,000; Harvard about $12,000; and Amherst less than $4,000; while the American Education Society received close to $14,000, the Presbyterian Society over $5,000, and the Baptist Society some $1,500.

We have pointed out that the ministry is the only calling for which training has thus far been subsidized in this way. The law, medicine, business, and technical pursuits have made their way by force of their economic importance to society. Has it been true that religion represents a " real " but not a " felt " need or has it been true, as Adam Smith would argue, that such procedure will overstock the occupation in question?

The actual demand for ministers is shown in a convincing manner by statistics published in the American Quarterly Register and in the annual reports of the societies.[38] That the demand was large is obvious from the fact that of all the graduates of 37 of the most prominent American colleges, from 20.8 per cent to 30.8 per cent entered the ministry in every five-year period between 1776 and 1865.[39]

Important as this profession was, the demand did not bring forth the supply, even with this special care. In this connection we must not overlook the fact that entrance to the ministry was by much longer educational route than was entrance to either the law or medicine, and without citing facts we know that it was not more remunerative than these other fields.

It follows then that something had to be done to meet the situation, and these education societies were the response which the churches made. With all the obvious waste the method involved, it not only did much toward the support of an important profession but it also supervised and helped to popularize the demand for higher education.

SUMMARY AND CONCLUSIONS.

In summarizing the development of this period we may note that the English influence practically disappeared with the Revolution and that State and National support continued.

Before the end of the period the idea of a State college had taken definite form, though the real burden still rested upon philanthropy. In nearly every State the church and private enterprise did the college pioneering.

Small gifts and the subscription method were as common as was the poverty which characterized the financial history of practically all the colleges of the period. Few, even of the older colleges, found themselves well endowed by 1861.

It was a period in which the old traditional college curriculum and organization yielded to the influence of the developments in science and to the broadening business and professional demands. Consequently, it was a time in which the conditions attaching to gifts were more numerous and perhaps more varied than in the past. In spite of this, there was a growing tendency to develop permanent funds.

These tendencies are as characteristic of the new as of the old foundations, and in both the conditional gifts tend to go mainly to professorships, library, and buildings; that is, to the institution rather than to the student direct. While there is some increase in interest in direct assistance for students, it is given, Princeton excepted, on the basis of scholarly promise rather than on that of indigence and piety.

---

[38] See an address of the board of education of the Presbyterian Church (their first annual report, 1819), p. 14; also their annual report for 1843, p. 5; and the same for 1867, p. 5.

[39] Burritt, p. 144.

The early financial history of the newer colleges of the period is identically like the beginning years of the old colonial group of colleges, but they grew much more rapidly.

During this period also we have the beginnings of several new ideas in higher education, which open up several new lines of philanthropic activity—the development of professional schools, women's colleges, church education societies, and the manual labor college.

In the development of schools of medicine, law, and theology we are struck by the fact that, from the standpoint of their scientific development, medicine and law achieved but little during this period and that very largely on the basis of private venture institutions, while theology was taken over by philanthropy and became well established, first as a department of the older colleges and later as separate schools. In the development of the theological schools denominationalism naturally played an important part, and the gathering of funds by the separate denominations from their own churches was the common practice.

Colleges for women offered a new motive for giving to education but nothing at all new by way of a method of directing the use to which gifts should be put.

When the law of supply and demand failed to provide enough ministers, philanthropy came at once to its rescue with education societies which played a large part in higher education during the period.

The manual labor college was the most unique though not the most valuable venture in higher education undertaken during the period. It failed, but it was an experiment that was fully warranted if we consider the times in which it was tried, and surely it is balanced by the success of women's colleges.

Whatever the value of the various experiments, it was philanthropy that initiated and carried them through, as it was mainly philanthropy that pioneered the new country and philanthropy that kept the old colleges alive through these years.

Chapter IV.
THE LATE NATIONAL PERIOD, 1865 TO 1918.

The period from 1865 to 1918 is quite unlike the colonial and early national periods in several ways. The rapid increase in population which began before the Civil War has continued, but has brought a foreign class far more difficult of assimilation than was that of pre-war days. With the rapid development of machinery have come remarkable industrial and commercial expansion and remarkable means of communication and travel. The free public land has fast disappeared, bringing with it a demand for new and technical methods in agriculture. The corporate method has been widely adopted, and large private fortunes have been amassed.

Along with these changes have come many new things in education. The idea of State support of higher education has been fully established; more than a dozen large private fortunes have given rise to as many institutions of higher learning; and some 8 or 10 large nonteaching foundations have been established. During this period a new interpretation of education has been developed in accordance with the findings of the newer sciences of sociology, psychology, and biology, and given concrete expression in the organization and methods of our institutions of higher education in the botanical garden, the laboratory method in all the sciences, in the free use of the elective system of studies, and in the broadened college entrance requirements.

GROWTH IN NUMBER OF COLLEGES.

Just how philanthropy has adjusted itself to these new conditions will now be shown. First of all, the relative number of colleges founded by philanthropy is a rough index of the extent, if not of the character, of its work.

At the beginning of this period the tendency to found private or church institutions was at its height, since which time the number has gradually decreased, till now very few are being established by either State or philanthropy, not so much because there are universities enough as because the changed meaning of education and the new conception of a university have ruled out the type of enterprise that tended to subsist on enthusiasm rather than on funds.

The new demands of this period have no more balked philanthropy than they have the State. If, however, consideration were given to the number of institutions that ceased to exist, it would be seen that philanthropy had very often overstepped its mark.

Soon after the Civil War, due very largely to the national land grant act of 1862, the movement for State schools began to assert itself.[1] Now all States have their higher institutions of learning, largely endowed by the National Government, but resting firmly upon a State tax.

---

[1] See Kandel, I. L. Federal Aid for Vocational Education. The Carnegie Foundation for the Advancement of Teaching, Bul. 10, 1917.

TABLE 17.—*Date of establishment and source of support and control of the first college or university in each of the States admitted subsequently to 1865.*

States.	Ad-mitted.	First institution.			State university or school estab-lished.	Number of colleges estab-lished before State univer-sity.
		Name.	Date estab-lished.	Control.		
Nebraska	1867	State University	1781	State	1871	0
Colorado	1876	University of Denver	1864	M. E	{ 1874 / 1877 }	2
North Dakota	1889	Jamestown College	1883	Presb	1884	1
South Dakota	1889	Yankton College	1881	Cong	1882	1
Montana	1889	Montana College of Agriculture	1893	State	1893	0
Washington	1889	State University	1861	State	1861	0
Idaho	1890	College of Idaho	1891	Presb	1892	1
Wyoming	1890	State University	1867	State	1867	0
Utah	1896	University of Utah	1850	State	1850	0
Oklahoma	1907	State Agricultural College	1891	State	1891	0
New Mexico	1912	State University	1891	State	1891	0
Arizona	1912	University of Arizona	1891	State	1891	0

Since 1865, 12 new States have been admitted to the Union. From Table 17 we are able to see that for the most part it was the State rather than philanthropy that did the pioneering in higher education in these States. In 9 of the 12 States higher education was well under way before the State was admitted to the Union. In 8 of the 12 States the first such school was established by the State, while in the remaining 4 the church lead the way, and in these 4 little had been done before the State institution was founded.

This contrasts rather sharply with the facts brought out in Table 9, which shows these same facts for the early national period. Here we are dealing with Western States, for the most part very sparsely settled, whereas Table 9 refers to Eastern and Central States, somewhat more densely populated. The chief explanation, however, would seem to be not that the missionary zeal of the churches, philanthropists, and educators was lagging, but rather that the idea of State higher education was getting under headway and that the national grant of 1862 came at an early date in the development of the West. The number of church and private foundations since established shows that the efforts of philanthropy have not flagged.

Should the State, or private and philanthropic enterprise, determine the character and amount of higher education? And related to this, what powers should be granted to private or church-endowed institutions? The struggle between these social theories, a notable early date in which is that of the Dartmouth College decision in 1819, does not begin in 1865. It began in one sense with the opposition in New Jersey Colony and elsewhere to sectarian control of the college which the colonial government was asked to help support. It began in a real sense in Revolutionary days and in the days when American democracy was taking form as a nation. At that time it was urged that, since higher education will do much toward determining national ideals, the State should direct and control it; and the opposite, that the State ought not to be taxed to send anyone's son to college. It is interesting that Presidents White, of Cornell, and Eliot, of Harvard, were on opposing sides of this issue at the beginning of this period.

Probably it is correct to say that this clash has provided the greatest stimulus to growth and expansion that has been felt by higher education through these years. This study can do little more than call attention here to these interesting theoretical developments.

GENERAL SURVEY OF EDUCATIONAL PHILANTHROPY IN THIS PERIOD.

Practically from its beginning in 1868 the United States Bureau of Education has included in its annual report statistics bearing upon the work of philanthropy in education. The following tables offer a fairly competent general picture of the extent and character of philanthropy in higher education since 1871. From Table 18 it is possible to see, at intervals of five years: First, the annual contribution to higher education from city, State, and Nation; second, the amounts contributed by students through tuition and other fees; third, the amounts contributed by productive funds held by the colleges; fourth, the contributions from philanthropy; fifth, the contributions from all other sources; and, finally, the total annual income of all institutions of higher education. Besides these is stated the wealth of the United States in billions of dollars, and the population by millions for each decade.

The steady increase in income from each of these sources as the years pass shows not only the rapid growth of higher education but the dependability of each of these sources of support. When the total column, or any single column, is compared with the growth in national wealth, it is plain that higher education is more liberally supported each succeeding decade. It will be noted that the "benefactions" column does not show the degree of increase that is shown by the first column or by the "total" column. This, however, is to be expected with the rise of the State colleges in this period. But it will be seen that benefactions are not quite keeping pace with the rate of growth in wealth. On the other hand, the rate of increase in wealth is surpassed by the growth in income from productive funds, most of which funds have been established by philanthropy.

In comparison with the growth in population, it is obvious that each decade is providing more educational facilities of a high order per unit of population than was provided by the next preceding decade. We have here to remind ourselves though that the per capita wealth has shown a far greater rate of increase than is shown by any of the other figures, which suggests that educational and philanthropic enthusiasms are not outrunning their purses.

TABLE 18.—*Sources and amounts of income for higher education in the United States, each fifth year from 1871 to 1915.*[1]

[Compiled from the annual reports of the U. S. Commissioner of Education.]

Dates.	From city, State, or U. S.	Tuition and other fees.	Productive funds.	Benefactions.	All other sources.	Total income.	Wealth of U. S. in billions of dollars.	Pop. of U. S. in millions.
1915.....	$36, 347, 638	$34, 067, 238	$18, 246, 427	$20, 310, 124	$9, 591, 784	$118, 299, 296	....	....
1910.....	24, 528, 197	19, 220, 297	11, 592, 113	18, 737, 145	6, 561, 235	80, 438, 987	187. 73	91. 9
1905.....	8, 522, 600	10, 919, 378	8, 618, 649	14, 965, 404	1, 589, 896	45, 715, 927	[2] 107. 10	....
1900.....	4, 386, 040	8, 375, 793	6, 110, 653	10, 840, 084	1, 964, 002	31, 676, 572	88. 51	75. 9
1895.....	2, 954, 483	6, 336, 655	5, 329, 001	5, 350, 963	2, 163, 499	22, 134, 601	[3] 77. 00	....
1890.....	1, 406, 117	3, 764, 984	3, 966, 083	6, 006, 474	1, 664, 734	16, 808, 734	65. 03	62. 9
1885.....	932, 635	2, 270, 518	3, 915, 545	5, 134, 460	. 1, 000, 000	12, 253, 158	....	....
1880.....	418, 159	1, 881, 350	3, 014, 048	2, 666, 571	10	7, 980, 138	42. 64	50. 1
1875.....	667, 521	2, 136, 062	2, 453, 336	2, 703, 650	....	7, 960, 569	....	....
1872.....	582, 265	4, 248, 143	2, 275, 967	6, 282, 461	....	13, 388, 836	[4] 30. 06	[4] 38. 5

[1] From 1871 this table includes universities and colleges for men and for both sexes; after 1905 technological schools are added; and after 1910 women's colleges are added.   Before 1888 column 1 includes income from State only; in 1890 it includes income from State and city; and after 1891 it includes income from States, cities, and United States.   Column 2 includes only tuition down to 1898, after which it includes "other fees" (board and room rent).   The figures in any given line, that is, for any given year, are fully comparable. In comparing the figures for one year or period with those of a later year or period, the above facts must be kept in mind.
[2] For year 1904.
[3] Estimated.
[4] For year 1870.

Table 19, covering the period from 1871 to 1885, including gifts to secondary as well as higher schools, shows that on an average more than half of all gifts have gone to "permanent endowment and general purposes." What part of this was available for immediate use it is not possible to determine; nor is it possible to say what were the special conditions placed upon the gifts.

TABLE 19.—*Total benefactions to all forms of education and the per cent of that total given under·the restrictions indicated.*

Dates.	Total benefactions.	Per cent given to—						
		Endowments and general purposes.	Professorships.	Fellowships, scholarships, and prizes.	Grounds, buildings, and apparatus.	Indigent students.	Libraries and museums.	Unconditional purposes.
1885	$9,314,081	58	7	2	20	1	2	10
1884	11,270,286	40	7	3	20	....	15	14
1882–83	7,141,363	45	7	3	15	2	2	26
1881	7,440,224	53	14	3	18	2	2	8
1880	5,518,501	54	15	7	12	2	3	7
1879	5,249,810	50	3	1	24	1	14	7
1878	3,103,289	57	4	4	16	3	6	10
1877	3,015,256	57	7	3	18	3	12	....
1876	4,691,845	38	5	3	32	....	15	7
1875	4,126,562	54	5	1	24	2	6	8
1874	6,053,804	68	2	1	21	2	2	4
1873	11,225,977	70	9	2	17	....	2	....
1872	10,072,540	23	6	1	34	1	....	....
1871	8,593,740	44	2	....	24	....	....	....

From a study of the "professorships" and the "fellowships, scholarships, and prizes" columns, which are not included in the "endowments and general purposes" column, it would be natural to infer that much of column two went to general unrestricted endowments. From the standpoint of growth in permanent endowment funds, however, the whole table, as a single sample of evidence, is quite reassuring. Furthermore, there is little to criticize in the evidence available on the nature of the conditions placed upon the gifts.

A fairly considerable amount has always been given unconditionally in the past, if we judge by individual cases which have been cited in the last two chapters, and here is evidence that this was true in general over the country through these 15 years. The "to indigent students" column seems to indicate that what was true in the early cases studied was also true in general.

In Table 20 is shown, from the same source, the distribution of gifts under three heads for the years 1907 to 1915, inclusive. Here there is no mistaking the evidence that generally over the country there is an increasing interest in giving to the permanent endowment of higher education. In this table the "endowments" column includes all gifts from which only the incomes can be used. By combining the three columns of Table 19 which represent gifts to permanent endowments, and assuming that "general purposes" in column one is also endowment, which is likely true, we can still see a clear indication that a larger percentage of gifts is going into permanent funds now than was true at the beginning of this period.

It appears also that the gifts to "plant and equipment" make a better showing in Table 20 than in Table 19. In both there is much fluctuation. The "current expenses" column, comparable with the last column of Table 19, shows improvement in quantity as well as a greater dependability.

A third collection of facts compiled from the United States Commissioner's reports and presented in the following tables furnishes evidence upon which we may generalize regarding the character and extent of benefactions to higher education through this period.

TABLE 20.—*Benefactions to higher education in the United States and the per cent of that total given for endowments, for plant and equipment, and for current expenses.*

Dates.	Total gifts.	Per cent for—		
		Endowments.	Plant and equipment.	Current expenses.
1915	$20,310,124	53	29	18
1914	26,670,017	69	18	13
1913	24,651,958	65	19	16
1912	24,783,090	59	26	15
1911	22,963,145	60	25	15
1910	24,755,663	39	50	11
1909	17,807,122	63	23	14
1908	14,820,955	50	35	15
1907	21,953,339	55	34	11

Table 21 shows the number of schools of theology, law, medicine, dentistry, pharmacy, agriculture, and mechanic arts, and of women's colleges that were opened during each five-year period since the first one was founded in 1761–1765. No account is taken here of colleges that have failed.

Three forces have assisted in the development of these schools—the State, philanthropy, and private enterprise. Philanthropy is almost, if not solely, responsible for the schools of theology. The State and private enterprise, with some help from philanthropy, have developed the law schools. All three are responsible for the medical schools, though private enterprise is playing a smaller and smaller part. Philanthropy has shown very little interest thus far in schools of dentistry and pharmacy, but has contributed liberally to colleges of agriculture and mechanical arts, which latter have been fostered mainly by the State. In most cases the State provides coeducational universities but not special schools for women.[2] The women's colleges included in this table are therefore the work of philanthropy and private enterprise.

Table 22 shows the part that philanthropy has taken in the development of these colleges.

The table is not complete, but one can not run up those columns without being impressed with the strength of the appeal which these fields of higher education have so continuously made to the people. Gifts for the higher education of women have increased with fair regularity and to a creditable extent.

---

[2] Florida State University has a separate college for women.

Table 21.—*Distribution of the present list (1915–16) of professional and technical and women's colleges with respect to the dates of their opening.*

Dates.	Theology.	Law.	Medicine.	Dentistry.	Pharmacy.	Agric. and mech. arts.	Women's colleges.
1761–1765			1				
1766–1779			1				
1781–1785	1		1				
1786–1790		1					
1791–1795	2						
1796–1800	1		1				
1801–1805						1	
1805–1810	2		1				
1811–1815	2	1	1				
1816–1820	5	1	2				
1821–1825	5		5				
1826–1830	6		1		1		1
1831–1835	4	3	2			1	2
1836–1840	4		3	1	1		5
1841–1845	4	1	6	1	1	1	5
1846–1850	6	4	6		1	1	7
1851–1855	7	2	1			1	16
1856–1860	13	4	5		1	4	15
1861–1865	7		2	1		4	2
1866–1870	18	9	4	4	3	8	11
1871–1875	9	7	4	1	2	9	8
1875–1880	3	5	4	5	2	4	4
1881–1885	14	4	3	5	7	3	5
1886–1890	8	6	5	9	5	5	9
1891–1895	14	16	9	8	15	8	8
1895–1900	5	15	5	7	13		6
1901–1905	9	10	10	6	11		8
1906–1910	3	14	6		5	1	2
1911–1915	3	15	3	1	6	1	
Total	155	119	92	49	75	52	114

Table 22.—*Benefactions to different lines of higher education in the United States each fifth year, 1871–1915.*

Dates.	Higher education of women.	Theological schools.	Medical schools.	National land-grant schools and schools of science.	Schools of law.
1915		$1,467,055	[1] $2,661,076		[2] $90,576
1910	$1,303,431	1,431,028	509,227		[3] 86,334
1905	1,107,523	[4] 1,890,606	354,210		
1900	588,566	1,123,812	183,500		105,500
1895	625,734	1,385,552	95,260		
1890	303,257	[5] 923,831	[5] 249,287	[5] $205,295	[5] 14,663
1885	322,813	681,855	94,250	562,371	[6] 40,150
1880	92,372	827,856	11,400	1,371,445	[7] 100,000
1875	217,887	404,356	72,395	147,112	
1871	1,600,000	652,265	2,000	285,000	

[1] In 1914 medical schools received $7,113,920.
[2] In 1914 law schools received gifts amounting to $203,067; in 1913, $189,453; in 1912, $425,867.
[3] In 1909 law schools received $356,800, and in 1908, $382,000.
[4] In 1906 theological schools received $3,271,480.
[5] In 1891.
[6] In 1886.
[7] In 1878.

Considering the steady decline in strictly sectarian theology through these years, and the general decline in religious zeal, gifts to theological schools have been large, as have all the others.

The column of gifts to medical schools shows the growth that has taken place in medical science as well as in medical education through this period. The same is, of course, not true of the theology column. In the absolute both theological and medical education have prospered. Both rise very slowly from the start, with slight advantage in favor of theological education down to 1890, and with this advantage slowly increasing from 1890 to 1909, after which medical education leaps far ahead.

Philanthropy, speaking now in relative terms, very definitely began to turn away from theology about 1890, and soon after to look with slightly more favor upon medical education. In the last decade these tendencies have become marked.

Turning again to Table 22 one is struck first by the immediate and liberal notice which philanthropists gave to the land-grant colleges and schools of science. The last column of the table is interesting in itself, and more so in comparison with the column showing gifts to medical schools. It is apparent here that society began to call a halt on apprenticeship methods of learning medicine before it did the same for law. Law has tended to remain much more a business than a profession, while the opposite is true of medicine and theology.

Taking these data from the Reports of the United States Commissioner of Education as a rough general picture of the educational philanthropy of this period, for it is dependable as such, one is impressed with the large contribution which has been made; with the apparent regularity or dependability of such sources of income; with the size, in the absolute, of the permanent sources which are thus being built up, but with the relative decline in such resources when all higher institutions of education are considered; with the relative increase in the amount of gifts to establish professorships; with the recent tendency toward increase in gifts to cover current expenses; with the regularity with which one-third to one-fifth of all gifts have gone to plant and equipment; with the rise, both relative and absolute, in the gifts to medical schools; with the corresponding decline in gifts to schools of theology; and with the relatively slow increase in gifts to schools of law.

STATUS OF EDUCATION AMONG ALL THE OBJECTS OF PHILANTHROPY.

Another source of data covering almost the last quarter century, and so almost half the period under discussion, is that contained in the Appleton and International Yearbooks and the World's Almanac. In these annuals there have been published the most complete available lists of all gifts of $5,000 and over, together with the object for which each was given. For some of the years these gifts have been classified under the following five heads: Educational institutions; charities; religious organizations; museums, galleries, public improvements; and libraries. Where they were not so classified the writer has been able to make such a classification with reasonable accuracy. In addition the gifts were also recorded as having been made by gift or by bequest, so that this classification was also possible. In these data, then, there is a valuable addition to the general description of philanthropy just presented.

111512°—22——5

TABLE 23.—*Distribution of the gifts and bequests recorded in the Appleton and New International Yearbook and the World's Almanac, 1893–1916.*

Years.	Amount of gifts and bequests.	Per cent of total given to—					Per cent in form of—	
		Education.	Charity.	Religious purposes.	Museums and public improvements.	Libraries.	Donations.	Bequests.
1893	$14,283,254	47	21	14	6	12	28	72
1894	15,976,466	43	20	11	17	9	17	83
1895	13,930,505	50	19	12	12	7	66	34
1896	13,831,211	50	16	19	9	6	48	52
1897	12,436,391	31	17	13	35	4	32	68
1898	20,405,034	57	25	7	7	3	54	46
1899	43,314,282	66	18	10	3	3	69	31
1900	23,690,473	54	27	7	5	7	55	45
1901	72,334,450	66	13	5	7	9	73	27
1902	55,174,640	60	21	6	8	5	49	51
1903	50,026,058	75	7	3	9	6	60	40
1904	24,918,399	45	29	9	14	3	30	70
1905	70,000,000	57	18	17	8	0	(1)	(1)
1906	29,775,000	79	15	4	2	0	83	17
1907	89,817,208	58	16	4	20	2	67	33
1908	46,552,039	40	44	4	10	2	48	52
1909	36,122,241	31	46	15	5	3	47	53
1910	61,283,182	43	38	8	6	5	70	30
1911	61,879,296	49	26	16	8	1	70	30
1912	35,207,907	16	76	4	3	1	74	26
1913	57,601,997	23	50	13	13	1	46	54
1914	90,741,210	45	48	2	4	1	67	33
1915	35,354,338	25	54	12	8	1	42	58
1916	72,612,619	9	88	2	1	½+	82	18
Total		34	49	7	8	2	64	36
Total with 1916 excluded		43	37	9−	9+	2	59	41

[1] Data inadequate.

This total column gives rather forceful evidence of the large part of the world's work that is being done by philanthropy. Through these 24 years the range is from 27 to 764 millions of dollars, with an average of nearly 125 millions. In 1915–16 the entire cost of public education in New York City was $45,010,424, and that for Chicago was $28,604,534. In this same year the total outlay for public education in the State of New York, which had the largest of all our State budgets for schools, was $68,761,125, while that for the United States was but $640,717,053. Again, the total income of all universities, colleges, and technological schools reporting to the United States Commissioner of Education in this year was $113,850,848.

If the huge gifts summarized in the table are flowing annually into the five channels indicated, we may see from these comparisons the large forces that are operating constantly to determine the character of the institutions of education, charity, and so on.

In considering the sum total of all benefactions, three questions deserve consideration. First, what is the relative position of education among the objects of these gifts; second, with what degree of regularity do these gifts come—that is, how dependable a resource does this make for education; and, third, how large a contribution is this to education? Incidentally, there is interest, too, in the same questions regarding gifts to other objects, especially to libraries and museums, since these play a direct part in the education of the people.

The first question is readily answered by Table 23, from which it will be seen that up to 1916 education was receiving annually from 16 to 79 per cent of these gifts, with a median of 49 per cent. When the figures for 1916 are included, and the totals taken for the 24-year period, it can be stated that education has received approximately 34 per cent of all gifts for the past 24 years. Or, leaving out 1916, as obviously influenced by war charity, education received 43 per cent of all gifts of $5,000 or over in the United States. The second question, how dependable is this source of income for education, may also be answered by this table, from which it is obvious that from year to year there have been wide variations. Consequently, an average or a median is not a full statement of the history of these benefactions, but the relative status of each of these recipients by years must be considered, and a number of points stand out. First, the facts about variability. What is true of education is true of the other objects. Second, giving to education gradually increased from 1893 to 1906, after which it declined to 1915 and 1916 to a point distinctly lower than the 1893 mark. At the same time the gifts to charity, which roughly maintain their 1893 status down to 1907, make a rise that is even sharper than is the decline in gifts to education. Gifts to religion have been quite variable, but show a general decline from the beginning to the end of the period. Practically the same statement can be made with respect to gifts to museums, galleries, and public improvements, with the exception that the variability is greater. The gifts to libraries show a very definite and regular decline from 1893 to 1916. It follows, then, that charity is education's great competitor, and we may be fairly sure that wars, famines, earthquakes, and other great disasters which appeal to human sympathy for help will be costly to education. The more recent rise in gifts to charity is partly accounted for by the Balkan and the World War and to several great earthquakes and fire disasters.

The third question, how large a help is this to education, is answered in Table 24, where the gifts to education and to libraries are set down beside the figures showing the total annual income to higher education in the United States. The annual income of higher education is used here merely as a convenient basis for measuring the amounts of the benefactions. From this we are able to see what the extent of philanthropy in education really is. To these educational benefactions might with some propriety be added those to libraries.

There is one other item of interest here, brought out in the last two columns of Table 23, viz, the extent to which these benefactions have preceded or followed the death of the donor. In 13 of the 23 years covered by the data a greater per cent has come by direct gift. Summing up the 23 years, the figures are 64 per cent by gift and 36 per cent by bequest. If 1916 is omitted, the figures are: Gifts, 59 per cent and bequests 41 per cent. The lowest per cent of gifts for any year was 17 in 1894 and the highest was 83 in 1906.

TABLE 24.—*Total benefactions to all forms of education in the United States, the total income for higher education in the United States as reported by the United States Commissioner of Education, and gifts to libraries.*

Years.	Benefactions to all forms of education.[1]	Total income of higher education.[2]	Benefactions to libraries.[1]
1916	$72,612,619	$133,627,211	$2,717,450
1915	35,354,338	118,299,296	916,000
1914	90,741,210	120,579,257	1,881,000
1913	57,601,997	109,590,855	2,162,000
1912	35,207,907	104,514,095	2,112,000
1911	61,879,296	94,672,441	1,942,500
1910	61,283,182	80,438,987	1,911,000
1909	46,122,241	76,650,969	3,012,293
1908	36,552,039	66,790,924	834,500

[1] From yearbooks above cited.
[2] From Reports of the United States Commissioner of Education.

TABLE 24.—*Total benefactions to all forms of education, etc.*—Continued.

Years.	Benefactions to all forms of education.	Total income of higher education.	Benefactions to libraries.
1907	$89,817,208	$68,079,616	$1,674,250
1906	29,775,000	57,502,280	
1905	70,000,000	45,715,927	
1904	24,918,399	41,618,228	961,100
1903	50,026,058	40,526,616	3,838,500
1902	55,174,640	39,952,798	4,045,500
1901	72,334,450	39,812,256	9,048,228
1900	23,690,473	31,676,572	3,270,000
1899	43,314,282	41,152,710	1,624,500
1898	20,405,034	26,745,610	942,500
1897	12,436,391	25,608,446	1,778,000
1896	13,831,211	26,260,902	1,535,000
1895	13,930,505	22,134,601	1,736,000
1894	15,976,466	24,390,852	3,912,713
1893	14,283,254	20,133,191	3,087,000

To the general picture then we may add, from the facts brought out here, that the general impressions gained from the data of the United States Commissioner's reports are reinforced at several points. Compared with the cost of education in the country, these gifts are of great consideration. Second, they have been, and there is reason to believe that they will continue to be, a dependable resource. Third, there is a definite decline in the amount of these gifts, which, however, seems to be explained by a corresponding rise in gifts to charity—charity so obviously demanded by the great catastrophes of the years of this decline. In addition, there is a decline in gifts to religion, to public improvements, and to libraries. With the exception of gifts to libraries, which have slightly declined in absolute amount, these declines are only relative, as may be seen from column three in Table 24. What should have caused this lessening of gifts to libraries is not evident from these figures. Carnegie's gifts extend from about 1881, and reports show no special decline in his gifts until very recently.

PHILANTHROPY AND THE OLDER COLLEGES.

Turning again to Tables 3, 4, and 6 for a more intensive study of philanthrophy as it affected three of our old colonial colleges, we are able to follow the tendencies through the present period.

Briefly stated, it may be noted that during this period no State support was received; that, looked at from any angle, the amounts of gifts have more than kept pace with their former record; that at Harvard and Columbia the earlier tendency to place a condition upon the gifts has continued, while at Yale the opposite has been true; and that gifts for permanent endowment show a relative decline at Harvard and Yale through this period, while at Columbia such gifts seem less popular than at Harvard, but more popular than at Yale.

Of the conditional gifts, it may be said that the " pious and indigent youth " has continued to fare less well throughout this period; that gifts for scholarships and fellowships have become more popular; that relatively (not in absolute amount) there has been a decline in gifts for professorships, except at Columbia; and that a still sharper relative decline in gifts to libraries has appeared. As to the form of gift, there is no special tendency anywhere toward gifts or bequests, except possibly at Yale, where bequests have increased.

Everywhere in these older institutions there is evidence of remarkable growth. Harvard is now well into the last quarter of its third century, and Columbia beyond the middle of its second century. There have been no more rapidly changing centuries in history than these. Surely these facts show that educational institutions founded and maintained by philanthropy can keep step with the passing years. If the "dead hand" had lain heavily upon these institutions, they would scarcely have maintained this rate of growth, either in toto or in the special lines here represented.

PHILANTHROPY IN COLLEGES OF THE EARLY NATIONAL PERIOD.

1. NEW LINES OF DEVELOPMENT.

In Chapter IV was described the work of philanthropy in a number of colleges which were founded during the early national period. Several new lines of development were begun in those years, notable among which were the beginnings of separate colleges for women, manual labor colleges, and separate schools of theology. It will be the purpose here to carry forward the study of several of those institutions.

It was said there that the philanthropy of that period was in the main directed by the various churches, and that in point of method the new colleges of those days originated and grew very much as did the colleges of the early colonial times.

2. AMHERST AS AN EXAMPLE OF THE COLLEGES OF LAST PERIOD.

Fairly complete data for Amherst College are presented in Tables 11 and 25. In Table 11 the Amherst data already discussed [2] have been carried forward to 1890. From this may be noted a continuance of most of the tendencies that had prevailed before the Civil War. The State did nothing more for the college, but the average annual income from gifts gradually increased. Most of the gifts were for a specified purpose, and among these, scholarships, professorships, and the library fared well. For some years after the Civil War the gifts were made immediately available, but endowments were favored from 1876 to 1890. The subscription method of obtaining gifts falls into disuse or nearly so, and as was true from the beginning, most of this income was by direct gift rather than by bequest.

In Table 25 is presented Amherst's income from "tuition and student fees," from "productive funds," and from "benefactions." This table covers the period 1895 to 1916, inclusive, at 4-year intervals, and brings out several interesting points. First, the amount from gifts fluctuates from year to year, roughly increasing up to the beginning of the World War and then declining. Income from tuition has also varied, but shows a substantial increase to the present, and income from permanent endowment funds has grown regularly, having more than doubled during the 22 years covered by the table.

TABLE 25.—*Income of Amherst College each fourth year, as reported by the United States Commissioner of Education.*

Dates.	Tuition and fees.	Productive funds.	Benefactions.	Total receipts.
1895	$42,000	$62,000	$30,000	$140,000
1899	50,000	50,000	65,000	165,000
1903	40,000	60,000	100,000	200,000
1907	37,500	90,000	78,000	210,500
1911	64,012	105,371	509,748	704,895
1915	59,957	139,982	30,552	237,834
1916	61,521	136,648	31,223	241,550

2 See p. 42 ff.

From these facts it is clear that if the college does not expand too rapidly, it will very soon be on a remarkably sound basis.

3. THEOLOGICAL INSTITUTIONS.

The growtn of Amherst is somewhat paralleled by that of Andover Theological Seminary, the early history of which has already been discussed.[4] Referring again to Table 12, it will be seen that after the Civil War, and down to 1890, Andover continued to receive contributions to her permanent funds, and that in increasing amounts. The details of these endowments are not all given in the table, but enough is shown to indicate that professorships, scholarships, and the library fared well.

According to reports of the United States Commissioner of Education, the total amount of Andover's permanent funds in 1872 was $550,000. With some fluctuations these funds have gradually increased to more than $810,000 in 1915. As early as 1852 these funds were furnishing an annual income of $35,000. By 1889 this had grown to $55,000, and it is recorded[5] that this was the entire income of the school for the year.

Here, then, is a theological school, founded in 1807, which has slowly built up an endowment fund that makes it virtually independent.

4. WOMEN'S COLLEGES.

As we have already seen,[6] Mount Holyoke College was one of the pioneer institutions devoted to the higher education of women. The school was founded and became well established in the second quarter of last century. The following tables will show something of its financial career since the close of the early national period.

Up to 1875 practically no permanent endowment funds had been accumulated. The school had in a very real sense been on trial[7] as a new philanthropic social project. That it fully proved its worth and received a large social sanction is shown by the figures of Table 26.

Column 1 of this table shows the total amount of permanent funds possessed by the college at intervals of five years from 1875 to 1915. In 1875 the college possessed a permanent fund of $50,000. In 1915 this had grown to near a million and a half dollars.

TABLE 26.—*Total endowment, total income, and sources of income for Mount Holyoke College at intervals of five years, 1875–1915.*[a]

Dates.	Total endowment.	Total income for the year.	Benefactions.	Income from—	
				Productive funds.	Tuition and other fees.
1875	$50,000	$48,000	....	$3,000	$45,000
1880	63,486	42,294	....	4,350	b 37,944
1885	103,600	55,500	....	7,500	b 48,000
1890	150,000	....	$19,000	....	....
1895	99,000	74,000	6,200	5,000	....
1900	475,000	139,663	31,000	24,061	115,602
1905	801,000	187,000	276,000	19,000	168,000
1910	838,750	279,721	31,292	34,666	100,197
1915	1,426,173	349,828	12,830	50,820	114,643

a Compiled from reports of United States Commissioner of Education.
b Includes board and tuition

4 See p. 44.
5 Rep. U. S. Commis. Educ., 1889.
6 See p. 45 ff.
7 A Boston paper refused to publish Miss Lyon's statements in behalf of the college unless paid for as advertising. Stowe, Hist. of Mount Holyoke Sem., sec. ed., 1887, p. 41.

It will be seen that permanent funds are rapidly assuming a larger and larger share in the annual income of the college, the main sources of which are also shown in this table. In 1875 the school received $3,000 from the income on permanent funds and $45,000 from student fees. In 1915 permanent funds produced $50,820 and tuition amounted to $114,643. This shows even more clearly what was mentioned above, and just what we have seen to be true of Andover and of Amherst, viz, that the rate of growth in income from permanent funds is greater than is the rate of growth in income from other sources. If this rate continues, it will not be many decades before philanthropy will have produced a college for women that will not be dependent upon student fees and that in spite of an extremely modest financial beginning.

No small part of Mount Holyoke's permanent funds are devoted to the general endowment of the college. The growth of this general fund, together with the permanent fund for scholarships, is shown in Table 27.

TABLE 27.—*Growth of two of Mount Holyoke's permanent funds, that for general purposes and that for scholarships.*[1]

Date.	Gifts to permanent fund for—		Date.	Gifts to permanent fund for—	
	General purposes.	Scholarships.		General purposes.	Scholarships.
Before 1875	$4,640	$26,666	1901–1905	$223,363	$14,000
1876–1880		7,000	1906–1910	5,500	19,500
1881–1885	25,000	22,500	1911–1915	432,750	56 314
1886–1890	50,792	10,000			
1891–1895	164,134	19,000	Total	1,091,179	218,480
1896–1900	185,000	43,500			

[1] Compiled from catalogues and the president's report.

From this table it appears that these two funds have increased rapidly and that each has reached a position of importance in the support of the college.

5. OBERLIN AN EXAMPLE OF THE MANUAL LABOR COLLEGE.

Oberlin College was another institution of the early national period whose early history has been traced.[8] It was pointed out that Oberlin's attempts at gathering funds for permanent endowment were pretty much a failure before the Civil War. Table 28 furnishes us with a very remarkable sequel, however, to that earlier story of hard times, for since the Civil War Oberlin has made progress quite similar to that noted above for Amherst, Andover, and Mount Holyoke.

It is not only in Oberlin's total, however, but in the purposes for which these totals were given that we see the large value of her endowment. This the table makes clear through a period of almost a half century.

[8] See p. 46 ff.

TABLE 28.—*Distribution of Oberlin's permanent funds, received by gift and bequest, 1833-1915.*[1]

Dates.	Total.	To general funds of—				Special funds.	
		University.	College.	Seminary.	Library.	Professorships.[2]	Scholarships.[3]
1860–1865	$6,000						$6,000
1866–1870	25,000					$25,000	
1871–1875	28,494	$17,514				8,935	2,045
1876–1880	96,291	1,286				91,005	4,000
1881–1885	464,093	186,026	$68,059	$42,135	$887	148,906	18,100
1886–1890	125,219			133	14,276	92,268	18,542
1891–1895	97,692		24,815	427		68,000	4,450
1896–1900	116,877		72,944		5,824	12,524	25,585
1901–1905	537,103	372,319	10,000	28,113	4,752	108,919	13,000
1906–1910	538,796	343,496	68,034	37,767	73,549	40,000	15,750
1911–1915	348,243	188,585	4,142	96,016			59,500

[1] Data for this table were compiled from the Oberlin General Catalogue, 1833-1908, and the Quinquennial Catalogue for 1916.

[2] Of the total amount of benefactions for this purpose to 1908, 51 per cent was received as direct gifts, 24 per cent by bequest, and 25 per cent by endowment canvasses. Nearly 26 per cent of it was for the endowment of religious and theological instruction and 18 per cent for instruction in natural and physical sciences.

[3] Of the total amount given for the endowment of scholarships during these years, 22 per cent was received by bequests, nearly 5 per cent came from churches, and 3 per cent from different classes of alumni. About 14 per cent of it was for those entering missionary work or those who were children of missionaries, more than 25 per cent was for indigent self-supporting students, 8 per cent for colored students, and 15 per cent for girls.

Some details concerning the growth of the professorship funds are added in Table 29. From these facts it appears that slightly more than half of the total of these funds was built up by subscription methods, approximately one-fourth by gift and the same by bequest.

TABLE 29.—*Date, amount, and source of each endowed professorship at Oberlin College.*

Dates.	Amount.	How obtained.	Branch of instruction endowed.
1867	$25,000	Bequest	Greek literature and archæology.
1875	8,935	Subscription	New Testament language and literature.
1877	21,371	....do	Old Testament language and literature.
1879	19,634	....do	Botany.
1880	50,000	Gift	Philosophy and psychology.
1881	25,000	....do	Homiletics.
1882	25,158	Subscription	Church history.
1882	23,748	....do	Economic and social science.
1882	30,000	Gift	Latin language and literature.
1884	25,000	Bequest	Mathematics.
1885	20,000	Gift	Physiology and physical training.
1889	55,881	Bequest	German and French.
1888	36,387	Subscription	Theology.
1893	38,000	Gift	Dean of women and director of women's gymnasium.
1895	30,000	....do	History.
1898	12,524	Subscription	Mediæval history.
1901	30,419	In part by subscription	Director of conservatory of music.
1902	40,000	Gift	Mineralogy and chemistry.
1904	38,500	Bequest	President's chair.
1907	40,000	Gift	Practical theology.

Considering these four colleges as fairly representative of the philanthropic foundations of the early national period, we may say of their development since the Civil War that in all cases this has been a period of rapid growth. The period of experimentation seems to have passed about war times, and these colleges to have been accepted as worthy of the full confidence of philanthropy. Permanent funds began to accumulate, slowly at first and then at an increasing rate, till now all have a substantial income from such funds.

At the present rate of growth, and with no more than normal expansion, these colleges will in time become practically independent of income from other sources. The endowment funds of these colleges are in large part available for general purposes, though considerable sums have been given for professorships, scholarships, and library.

PHILANTHROPY IN THE COLLEGES OF THIS PERIOD.

Down to 1865 practically every college had begun its existence with very small funds, usually with little or no real endowment, and had had to pass through a long financial struggle before it had won a clientage sufficient to guarantee its future. During the period here under discussion colleges continued to be founded on that same basis. Drury College began in poverty in 1873 and remained poor until 1892, when a gift of $50,000 laid the foundation of her present endowment of over a quarter of a million. Carleton College, chartered in 1867, began with $20,000 received from the citizens of Northfield and $10,000 received from the Congregational Churches of the State. In 1915 this college possessed endowment funds of almost a million dollars. Washburn College, chartered in 1865, was started by small gifts from the Congregational Churches, but by 1915 had developed an endowment of over $360,000. These are but three from the many well-known illustrations of this type.

1. THE PRIVATELY ENDOWED UNIVERSITY A NEW TYPE.

In addition to this type, however, we see the beginning of a new era in educational philanthropy—an era in which a great and independently endowed university could spring into existence almost at once from the gifts of a single benefactor.

Such schools did not have to go to the public and beg for funds, nor await any sort of social sanction. They secured their charters as corporations, erected their buildings, called together their faculties, organized their curricula, and opened their doors to students. They start, therefore, as educational and philanthropic, and we might also say, social experiments. Can such financially powerful corporations be trusted to keep faith with America's educational, economic, religious, and social ideals was the question in many minds at that time.

An examination of the charters, articles of incorporation, and other foundation documents of these institutions should reveal something of their own conception of what their function was to be. Accordingly the following excerpts from these sources are presented:

1. EDUCATIONAL AIMS.

The charter of Vassar College was issued in 1861. Section 2 of this charter declares it to be the object and purpose of the corporation " To promote the education of young women in literature, science, and the arts."

A fuller statement is to be found in Matthew Vassar's address to the trustees of the college, delivered on February 26, 1861, in which he says:

I wish that the course of study should embrace at least the following particulars: The English language and its literature; other modern languages; the ancient classics, as far as may be demanded by the spirit of the times; the mathematics, to such an extent as may be deemed advisable; all the branches of natural science, with full apparatus, cabinets, collections, and conservatories for visible illustrations; anatomy, physiology, and hygiene, with practical reference to the laws of health of the sex; intellectual philosophy; the elements of political economy; some knowledge of the Federal and State Constitutions and laws; moral science, particularly as bearing on the filial, conjugal, and parental relations; æsthetics, as treating of the beautiful in nature and art, and to be illustrated by an extensive gallery of art; domestic economy, practically taught, so far as possible, in order to prepare graduates readily to become skillful housekeepers; last, and most important of all, the daily, systematic reading and study of the Holy Scriptures as the only and all-sufficient rule of Christian faith and practice.[*]

Cornell's charter, granted in 1865, says, in section 3:

The leading object of the corporation hereby created shall be to teach such branches of learning as are related to agriculture and the mechanical arts, incuding military tactics; in order to promote the liberal and practical education of the industrial classes in the several pursuits and professions in life. But such other branches of science and knowledge may be embraced in the plan of instruction and investigation pertaining to the university as the trustees may deem useful and proper.[10]

In addition to this statement from the charter, we have the following words from Ezra Cornell, the founder:[11]

I hope we have laid the foundation of an institution which shall combine practical with liberal education, * * * I desire that this shall prove to be the beginning of an institution which shall furnish better means for the culture of all men, of every calling, of every aim; * * * training them to be more useful in their relations to the State, and to better comprehend their higher and holier relations to their families and their God.

Finally, I trust we have laid the foundation of a university—" an institution where any person can find instruction in any study."

Johns Hopkins says in his will:

I do hereby give, devise, and bequeath all the rest * * * of my real and personal estate to be held, used, and applied by such corporation in, for, and to its corporate purposes in accordance with the provision of its existing charter of incorporation, etc.[12]

In this brief and formal certificate of incorporation of August 24, 1867, we find the general declaration of purpose to be that of " Organizing a university for the promotion of education in the State of Maryland," etc.[13]

These general ideas of the purpose of Johns Hopkins University are made a bit more specific in the inaugural address of the first president in which he lays down 12 principles fairly well expressed in the following brief excerpts:[14]

1. All sciences are worthy of promotion, etc.
2. Religion has nothing to fear from science, and vice versa.
3. Remote utility is quite as worthy to be thought of as immediate advantage.
4. As it is impossible for any university to encourage with equal freedom all branches of learning, a selection must be made by enlightened governors, and that selection must depend on the requirements and deficiencies of a given people in a given period.
5. Teachers and pupils must be allowed great freedom in their method of work.

In his next several principles he lays emphasis upon the importance of a broad liberal culture for all students; upon research for professors, upon the influence of research upon instruction, and vice versa; points out that honors must be bestowed sparingly and benefits freely; and says that a university is a thing of slow growth and very liable to fall into ruts.

---

[*] In *Vassar*, by Taylor, James Monroe, and Haight, Elizabeth Hazelton, Appendix II.
[10] Cornell University Register, 1868.
[11] Founder's Address at the inaugural of President White in 1868, in Biography of Ezra Cornell, A. S. Barnes & Co., 1884, p. 199 ff.
[12] Johns Hopkins University—Charter, Extracts of Will, Officers, and By-Laws. Baltimore, 1874.
[13] Published with subsequent amendments in the University Register for 1918–19.
[14] Addresses at the Inauguration of Daniel C. Gilman, as President of Johns Hopkins University, Baltimore, 1876.

The founding grant of Leland Stanford Junior University declares that it is "Its object to qualify its students for personal success and direct usefulness in life."

And further:

Its purposes, to promote the public welfare by exercising an influence in behalf of humanity and civilization, teaching the blessings of liberty regulated by law, and inculcating love and reverence for the great principles of government as derived from the inalienable rights of man to life, liberty, and the pursuit of happiness.

In addition to work of instruction, the university was designed "to advance learning, the arts, and sciences."

In the University of Chicago certificate of incorporation we find the aim of the foundation expressed in section 2 as follows:

To provide, impart, and furnish opportunities for all departments of higher education to persons of both sexes on equal terms; * * * to establish and maintain a university in which may be taught all branches of higher learning.

Such are the educational aims of these institutions as they were conceived by the founders.

2. RELIGIOUS AIMS.

The religious emphasis is shown to some extent in these same documents.

Vassar's charter makes no reference to religion, but Mr. Vassar, in the address above quoted, does. In addition to the reference to religion in the above quotation, he says:

All sectarian influences should be carefully excluded; but the training of our students should never be intrusted to the skeptical, the irreligious, or the immoral.

Cornell's charter makes specific reference to religion, as follows:

SEC. 2. But at no time shall a majority of the board be of any one religious sect or of no religious sect.

SEC. 3. And persons of every religious denomination shall be equally eligible to all offices and appointments.

In Johns Hopkins' brief charter no reference is made to religion, but in President Gilman's address, as above quoted, we can see that questions of religion were to fix no limitations in the life of the university at any point.

Leland Stanford's foundation grant as amended in October, 1902, says:

The university must be forever maintained upon a strictly nonpartisan and nonsectarian basis.

The charter of the University of Chicago says:

SEC. 3. At all times two-thirds of the trustees and also the president of the university and of said college shall be members of regular Baptist Churches * * * in this particular this charter shall be forever unalterable.

No other religious test or particular religious profession shall ever be held as a requisite for election to said board or for admission to said university * * * or for election to any professorship or any place of honor or emolument in said corporation, etc.

Such aims as these could not have been expressed in earlier college charters. The idea of educating young women in the sciences; the idea of connecting science as taught in the college with the work of the farmer and mechanic; the laboratory method of teaching; the idea of investigation and research as a university function; the slight general references to and the broad liberality in matters of religion; these things could not have been written into the foundation documents of our colonial colleges. There is a marked contrast between the general tone and the actual ideas and ideals expressed here and those shown from colonial charters in Table 1 above.

The new education is strongly suggested in almost every line of these documents, and a careful analysis of the conditions placed upon the foundation gifts would show that very little is to be subtracted from the showing which the above quotations make.

Mr. Rockefeller demanded that the Baptist Education Board should raise $400,000 to put with his gift of $600,000, his gift to become a permanent endowment for current expenses. The conditions of his next several large gifts were quite as simple.

Matthew Vassar placed in the hands of his trustees securities worth $400,000 with which to build a seminary and college for women. He explained what his notion of such a college was and then very modestly advised the board as to future use of the funds.

Mr. Cornell had to meet the demands—not altogether reasonable—of the State of New York, and those of the national land-grant act of 1862 before he could give $500,000 to build a university.

These are typical. These great fortunes were to build and endow a " college " or a " university," as the case might be, and no narrow limitations were placed upon the use of the gifts to those ends. With such large initial funds available, it is obvious that these institutions are in a position to reject any subsequent gift that does not meet the essential purposes for which the schools were founded. The aims laid down in their charters can be carried out without help if necessary,[15] and it is especially noteworthy, therefore, that in no case has society failed to accept the foundation in the right spirit. Almost from the start the people made these projects their own, as was evidenced by the contributions which very soon began to flow into their treasuries from outside sources.

3. TYPES OF EARLY CONDITIONAL GIFTS.

Vassar College.—Vassar College was founded in 1861 and was opened to students in 1865. Mr. Vassar's first gift was $408,000. In 1864 he added a gift of $20,000, for an art collection, and in 1868, by his will, he canceled a $75,000 debt for the college, and added $275,000 to establish a lectureship fund, a students' aid fund, a library and art cabinet fund, and a repair fund. The first important gift to come to Vassar from the outside was in 1871, when A. J. Fox gave $6,000 to establish the Fox scholarship. This was soon followed by two other gifts for scholarships and in 1879 by a gift of $6,000, and in 1882 by another of $3,000, both for scholarships.[16]

In 1879 two of the founder's nephews agreed to build a laboratory of chemistry and physics; in addition to which Matthew Vassar, jr., gave $50,000 for scholarships and $40,000 for two professorships. In 1890 an endowment fund of $100,000 was raised by subscriptions.[17]

---

[15] Andrew D. White, in his Autobiography, Vol. I, p. 413, quotes the following statement from a trustee of Johns Hopkins University : " We at least have this in our favor ; we can follow out our own conceptions and convictions of what is best ; we have no need of obeying the injunctions of any legislature, the beliefs of any religious body, or the clamors of any press ; we are free to do what we really believe best, as slowly and in such manner as we see fit."

[16] In accepting some of these scholarships the college bound itself for all time to educate a girl on each of the foundations. That was possible when money was worth 7 per cent, and the cost of such education $400 ; but as money fell to 4½ to 5 per cent, and the cost of such education rose to $500, such gifts became liabilities in place of assets. This, however, was no fault of philanthropy, but due rather to shortsighted management on the part of the college. Such management was not, however, without precedent. See discussion of Oberlin scholarships, p. 46.

[17] These facts were taken from Tailor and Haight's Vassar, and from President's Reports and Catalogues.

This covers practically all the gifts to Vassar during its first 25 years of work. Certainly the conditions named have been in line with the main purposes of the founder.

Cornell University.—At Cornell University, founded in 1865, we have a somewhat different situation. The half million dollar gift of the founder was very thoroughly bound to fulfill certain conditions laid down by the State legislature.[18] The university started and grew against serious opposition of almost every sort, and almost immediately gifts began to be received.

In 1871 Henry W. Sage gave $250,000 to establish and endow a women's college; John McGraw erected the McGraw Building, at a cost of about $100,000; Hiram Sibley presented a building and equipment for the college of mechanic arts at a cost of over $50,000; President White built the President's House, at a cost of some $60,000; and Dean Sage endowed the chapel which had been built by a gift of Henry W. Sage. These are typical of many other early gifts which produced a phenomenally rapid growth of the university.[19]

John Hopkins University.—Johns Hopkins opened its doors in 1876, having been chartered in 1867. Almost immediately its large foundation began to be supplemented by gifts and bequests. In his will, dated February 26, 1876, Dr. Henry W. Baxley left $23,836 to found a medical professorship. In the same year a small gift was received for a scholarship, and this was followed by several others during the next few years. Large and important book collections, including a large German law library for Heidelberg, were contributed to the library very soon after it was opened, and two $10,000 fellowships were contributed in 1887. Numerous small gifts are also recorded, but these are fully typical of the conditional gifts to Johns Hopkins during her first two decades.[20]

Chicago University.—Among the early gifts to the University of Chicago after it was chartered in 1890 was a site for the college by Marshall Field and a million-dollar gift from Mr. Rockefeller, $800,000 of the latter to be used as a permanent fund for the support of nonprofessional graduate instruction and fellowships, $100,000 to be used as a permanent fund for the endowment of theological instruction in the divinity school of the university, and $100,000 to be used in the construction of buildings for the divinity school. In 1891 the trustees of the William B. Ogden estate began proceedings which ended in a gift of nearly $600,000 for the Ogden Graduate School of Science. In 1893 Silas B. Cobb gave a $150,000 recitation building, and in this same year three other large gifts for buildings were received. Numerous other gifts, such as an astronomical observatory, a physical laboratory, a chemistry building, an oriental museum, followed within a few years, as also did large sums for endowment.

Leland Stanford Junior University.—At Leland Stanford Junior University, opened in 1891 on the largest initial foundation gift yet made to an American institution of higher learning, numerous valuable gifts were made to the library and museum from the start. The half-million dollar jewel fund for the endowment of the library was the gift of Mrs. Stanford in 1905. Other large gifts from Thomas Welton Stanford restored the museum, which had been destroyed by the earthquake in 1906, and added an art museum and a

[18] By the charter the university was made subject to visitation of the regents of the University of New York, and the trustees were made personally liable for any debt above $50,000. It also made the founding gift of Mr. Cornell absolutely unconditional.
[19] For these facts, see President White's Autobiography, and W. T. Hewett's Cornell University, a History, Vol. III, Appendix.
[20] See A List of Gifts and Bequests Received by the John Hopkins University, 1876–1891, Baltimore, 1892.

valuable art collection. Several prize scholarship, fellowship, and lectureship funds were also among the early gifts.

We may say, then, that these institutions did receive gifts from the outside, and that very soon after they were founded. We may say that the conditions of these gifts were unquestionably in accord with the essential aims set forth in the charters of the schools. In other words, these projects met the real test and passed it, and having received society's sanction they have joined the ranks of Harvard, Yale, Columbia, Oberlin, Amherst, and the long list of institutions which these names suggest.

4. ANALYSIS OF GIFTS TO TWO UNIVERSITIES OF THIS GROUP.

It is possible to add to this description something of the financial history of two of these universities. Tables 30 and 31 give us a fairly complete account of the income to the University of Chicago and to Cornell University at intervals of five years down to 1915. Any one of the columns of these tables is instructive. All point to the phenomenal growth of these universities. The income from tuition shows the rapid growth of the student bodies, and when compared with the column showing the total income it is seen that throughout Cornell's history tuition has furnished from one-fourth to one-seventh of the total annual income, while at the University of Chicago this percentage is from one-third to one-fifth. The income from productive funds in both tables shows a steady and rapid increase almost from the start, and at Cornell has furnished from two to six and even nine times the income produced by tuition.

The gifts column in Table 31 shows that gifts have become, subsequently to 1890, an extremely important and dependable source of income. It should be added that an examination of the treasurer's reports shows that a large percentage of these gifts to Cornell have been going into the permanent funds of the university.

In Table 30 we have a further analysis of the benefactions to the University of Chicago after 1906, from which we are able to see the extent to which gifts are being received for enlargement of plant, for endowment, and for current expenses, respectively, from which it is evident that a very large percentage of all gifts go into the permanent funds.

TABLE 30.—*Income of University of Chicago at 5-year intervals from 1890 to 1915.*[1]

Dates.	From student fees.		From productive funds.	From private benefactions for—			From other sources.	Total income.
	Tuition.	Other student fees.		Plant.	Endowment.	Current expenses.		
1890.........								
1895.........	$130,000		$140,000		$2,127,083		$205,000	$1,365,000
1900.........	294,402		207,620		1,563,695		30,280	2,095,997
1905.........	504,554		336,144	[2] $1,634,910	579,873	[2] $388,270	47,607	1,468,178
1910.........	588,721	193,989	774,246	273,642	867,048	53,635	46,687	2,793,968
1915.........	708,175	217,838	1,094,254	352,193	784,303	7,885	103,880	3,268,508

[1] Data compiled from United States Commissioner's Reports and from the reports of the university president.
[2] In 1907.

TABLE 31.—*Financial exhibit of income of Cornell University at five-year intervals from 1865 to 1915.*[1]

Years.	Tuition fees.	Other receipts from students.	Income of investments.	Productive funds.	All other sources.	Total.
1865–66						$9,000
1868–69	$33,348			$130,000		76,744
1874	15,105	$1,993	$80,000		$9,203	106,301
1879	18,545	1,637	73,662		13,314	107,158
1884	17,050	2,719	186,907		10,700	217,377
1889	46,000	18,502	275,028		22,775	362,304
1894	114,277	26,736	314,993	112,595	55,931	624,531
1899	155,003	38,413	376,033	64,855	40,849	675,153
1904	251,031	57,311	413,629	485,449	122,915	1,330,336
1909	476,400		428,562	183,252	119,624	1,460,610
1914	535,346	45,334	644,637	4,376,103	346,595	6,790,260
1915	622,575	183,975	709,777	201,484	409,826	3,161,381

[1] Data to 1904 from Hewett's Cornell University, and subsequent to 1904 from Reports of the United States Commissioner of Education.

From these figures it is evident that the scale upon which these institutions were founded has been fairly maintained as their scale of growth. Chicago's income from permanent funds is furnishing an increasing proportion of her annual income, while the opposite appears to be true of Cornell. The latter is explained by the fact that Cornell has in recent years been receiving relatively large annual appropriations from the State, the city, and the United States. What we have noted above regarding the endowment funds of the colonial and early national colleges, then, is equally true of these younger institutions. They are rapidly building up a source of support that will, under normal expansion, make them independent.

If we ask regarding the further conditions placed upon these vast gifts to higher education, we have but to read over the lists published in the yearbooks, in magazines, and in official university publications to see that they are rarely out of line with the main lines of growth in the institution receiving them. More than half of Cornell's permanent funds belong to the general funds of the university or to some one of the schools or departments.[21]

Of the great foundations of this period then we may say: Financially they are practically independent from the start; each is, in the main, the gift of one man; their charters grant them almost unlimited freedom to become anything they may choose to call college or university; they are very definitely nonsectarian and nonpolitical, but one, Chicago, is definitely fostered by a church; they cultivate liberality in matters of religion; they stress original research as a professorial function; and, in the face of real opposition in some cases, as well as the natural tendency to distrust such large corporations, the gifts they have received from the start show that they have been accepted by the public as fully as have the most ancient or most religious foundations of the past. All are rapidly building up permanent endowment funds which promise a large degree of financial independence in the future, and, judged by our best standards, all are not only fully law-abiding, but each in its own way is exercising wide leadership in the field of higher education.

PHILANTHROPY THROUGH RELIGIOUS EDUCATION SOCIETIES.

As explained in Chapter III, religious education societies arose very early in the last century in response to a growing demand for trained ministers,

---

[21] A full list of these funds with date and amount of each, and with fairly complete statement of conditions controlling the use of their income, is published in the annual report of the treasurer for 1915–16.

which demand the colleges were failing to meet. They organized and were chartered as corporations to aid in the education of young men for this calling. They operated mainly by direct aid to the student, though in some cases grants were made to colleges. Most of the societies did some work of this kind, even going so far as to found colleges in some instances.[22]

Most of these societies survived the period of the Rebellion and have continued, separately or in combination, to carry on this work to the present time. Many other societies have also been organized, several new ones having appeared very recently. The old methods of assistance have continued in force, and permanent endowment funds have in several cases grown to importance, and it is plain that the influence of these organizations is becoming greater. At present they are organized on denominational lines, though originally many of them were not so.

1. THE AMERICAN EDUCATION SOCIETY.

Something of the extent of their service to higher education may be seen from the following tables, which are typical of the best work that is being done by these societies. Table 32 shows the annual income of the American Education Society, the number of students assisted, the amount of permanent funds possessed, the total annual grant to colleges, and, for a few years, the number of colleges receiving these grants. The first two columns are a continuation of columns one and two in Table 14.

TABLE 32.—*Financial statistics of the American Education Society at intervals of five years from 1866 to 1915.*

Dates.	Amount received.	Students aided.	Amount of permanent fund.	Grants to colleges.[1]	Colleges aided.
1865	$21,613	253	$81,000		
1870	27,120	354	81,500		
1875	93,713	413	81,500	[2] $62,375	8
1880	64,097	367	83,499	38,983	11
1885	60,124	309	103,418	[3] 88,137	[3] 8
1890	101,425	359	112,622	58,336	
1895	141,189	335	225,342	26,534	
1900	120,047	138		28,861	
1905	144,036	192	281,114	7,849	
1910	129,555	231	282,124	22,731	
1915	89,639			10,521	4

[1] Usually much larger sums were given to academies than to colleges.
[2] In this year (1875) the society joined with the Society for the Promotion of Collegiate and Theological Education, was chartered, and became the American College and Education Society.
[3] In 1884.

If we turn to Table 14 we will see that this society grew rapidly from its beginning in 1815 to well into the thirties, after which it slowly declined until after the Civil War, when it again entered upon a period of prosperity which has continued practically to the present time.

In 1874 the American Education Society, which had worked mainly by grants to students, was combined with the Society for the Promotion of Collegiate and Theological Education in the West, which had operated by making grants to colleges.[23] This shift in emphasis appears in column 4 under " grants to colleges."

The rise in income along with the decline in number of students and colleges aided is explained by the fact that increasing attention has been given to the

---

[22] As when the Western College Society founded Illinois College   1843.
[23] See p. 50 ff.

work of academies, pastorates, and missionary schools.[24] The society has not only prospered, but its total service to education has increased.

2. THE PRESBYTERIAN EDUCATION BOARD.

Table 33 continues for the board of education of the Presbyterian Church the facts shown for that society in Table 14. In addition, this table shows the number of churches from which contributions were received, and the maximum amount and the total amount of aid granted to students.

TABLE 33.—*Financial statistics of the Presbyterian Board of Education at intervals of five years.*[1]

Years.	Number of contributing churches.	Receipts from all sources.	Number of candidates aided.	Maximum amount of aid.	Total amount paid to candidates.
1866		$46,751	296		$41,027
1870		52,276	391	$150	40,897
1875		68,179	496	150	63,450
1880	2,208	55,649	424	100	40,861
1885	2,632	72,733	619	110	63,314
1890	3,008	84,936	839	100	67,651
1895	3,165	97,278	1,031	80	79,071
1900	3,523	77,763	716	80	51,499
1905	3,788	119,104	658	100	64,535
1910	4,958	148,503	843	100	81,414
1915	5,431	164,459	776	75–150	79,815
1917	5,504	203,592	895	75–150	86,902
Total		4,864,402			3,147,537

[1] Statistics from the 98th An. Rep. of the board, in 1917; the Cumberland Presbyterian Education Society united with this board in 1906; their first joint report is in 1907.

First of all, it will be seen that since 1878 the number of churches contributing to the funds of this society has practically trebled. This increase in the society's clientage has been very gradual, and an examination of the receipts shows that the average contribution per church has remained fairly constant or perhaps increased slightly. If we examine the three last columns of this table we see that its service has also increased. The number of students aided has increased from 296 in 1866 to 1,037 in 1896; then, after a decline for a few years, has risen again to 895 in 1917. During these years the amount of aid per student has fluctuated somewhat but on the whole has declined, while the total of grants has varied somewhat with the number of students aided.

3. METHODIST EPISCOPAL CHURCH BOARD.

The board of education of the Methodist Episcopal Church took definite form in 1864. Its charter empowered it to aid young men desiring to enter missionary work or the ministry, and to aid biblical or theological schools, as well as universities, colleges, and academies then (1869) under the patronage of the church. No gifts were to be made for buildings and no aid was to be given to any school not then in existence, except "the board shall first have been consulted and shall have approved of the establishment and organization of such institution."[25] Down to 1908 it has rendered aid to higher education

[24] See An. Rep. of the Treasurer, 1916.
[25] See the original charter of 1869, published in the 1904 report.

entirely by making loans direct to students, for the reason that it had practically no funds for work of a broader scope.[26] Since that time it has, in addition to this, made grants to colleges. Table 34 shows the annual receipts from gifts, the annual outlay in the form of loans to students, the annual grants to institutions, and, for some years, the number of students receiving these loans. From these figures it is evident that this society has made a remarkably rapid growth. From its beginning in 1873 to 1915 the board claims to have assisted a total of 22,392 different students.[27] That includes those in the academies and theological schools as well as those in college.

TABLE 34.—*Financial statistics of the board of education of the Methodist Episcopal Church, 1868–1915, at intervals of five years.*[1]

Years.	Amount received less interest on permanent funds.	Amount of loans to students.	Number of students aided.	[1]Amount of aid to institutions.
1868	$84,000			
1875	2,141	$10,095		
1880	5,079	8,000		
1885	38,852	31,684		
1890	64,914	42,173		
1895	76,529	70,596	1,540	
1900	114,651	81,749		
1905	130,640	108,658		
1910	164,608	115,400	2,072	$20,496
1915	200,158	123,696	2,189	43,528
Total	3,338,725	2,634,034		260,072

[1] Compiled from annual and quadrennial reports of the board.

TABLE 35.—*Biennial receipts of the board of education of the Evangelical Lutheran Church in the United States of America.*

Periods.	Amount received.	Periods.	Amount received.	Periods.	Amount received.
1887–1889	$6,409	1897–1899	$21,012	1907–1909	$104,866
1889–1891	10,140	1899–1901	27,070	1909–1911	88,859
1891–1893	14,181	1901–1903	41,105	1911–1913	75,656
1893–1895	15,288	1903–1905	40,635	1913–1915	89,746
1895–1897	19,878	1905–1907	54,234	1915–1917	95,738

4. EVANGELICAL LUTHERAN CHURCH BOARD.

In 1885 the board of education of the Evangelical Lutheran Church in the United States of America was organized and has operated continuously since. Table 35 shows the resources of the board biennially since its foundation. Its method of work has been that of making contributions to various educational institutions. According to treasurers' reports, gifts to colleges were sometimes for the " budget " of the school and sometimes for a specific item, as interest on a debt, special endowment, scholarship, etc. For the past decade reports show that at least seven institutions were regular recipients of aid from this board, and it appears from reports to have been responsible for founding, and also for refusing to found, new institutions, which together indicates that it is in some sense a supervising agency.

[26] See discussion of this in the annual report of the board for 1904.
[27] An. Rep., 1910.

5. WORK OF THESE SOCIETIES EVALUATED.

While it is not possible to state just what proportion of the funds of these societies has gone into higher education, it is clear that all effort has been aimed directly or indirectly at training for the ministry. One has but to glance at the columns, and especially at their totals, to realize that these organizations have meant much to the growth of higher education in this country. The income of the Presbyterian board for 1917 is approximately that of such colleges as Wells and Beloit.

The showing for these four societies or boards is probably typical of the best that is being done by these organizations. Undoubtedly thousands of young men and women have received secondary or collegiate training who would otherwise have received little or no schooling. The ministry has brought many into its service by this means. These societies have saved colleges which were virtually bankrupt. By small gifts they have stimulated much larger ones. They have exercised supervision over colleges under their patronage by refusing aid to those which show no promise. They have by these and other means attempted standardization, and it should be added that the Methodist board began to exercise this influence very early.[28] They have through church pulpits and Sunday schools brought the problems of college education to the attention of a large percentage of our population. More recently coordination of the efforts of these many boards, through the work of the council of church boards of education, is resulting in a more intelligent placement of new foundations. Doubtless we should add that these boards have helped to save denominationalism among churches, whatever that may be worth.

Most of them seem to be worthy aims, if the cost has not been too great. In opposition to this kind of philanthrophy it is sometimes argued that a young man who is put through college by the aid of these boards naturally feels obligated to enter the ministry regardless of the fact that he discovers in the course of his training that he is better fitted for some other calling; that, as a rule, academy students are not in a position to decide upon a vocation; that the scholarship method, unless appointments are based upon ability, is not the best way to stimulate scholarly efforts; and that the cost of administering the funds is too large.[29]

It is clear at any rate that these boards are occupying a much stronger position among the churches than formerly. Their supervision is real supervision, when it is possible for them to close up such of their own weaker insti-

---

[28] In 1892 general conferences of the Methodist Episcopal Church authorized a "university senate" to formulate a standard of requirements for graduation to baccalaureate degree in their church schools, and the board was authorized to classify as colleges only such schools as met those requirements. See Appendix to Annual Report for 1892, and for the general conference for 1896, p. 736. The colleges are classified on this basis in the annual reports of the board for 1895.

[29] In 1875 approximately 11 per cent of the expenditures of the American College and Education Society was for the cost of administration. The cost of administration for the Methodist board amounted to more than 16 per cent of the total expenditures in 1889, and about 27 per cent in 1915, and the same figure for the Presbyterian board in 1888 was about 10 per cent. Of course these are only rough figures. The administrative officers are often engaged in ways that are directly useful in the development of higher education. The application of college standards by the administrative officers of the Methodist board is a fair illustration. The making of educational surveys, the gathering and publication of educational information, the vast amounts of correspondence in connection with gifts and loans, and the advice to colleges concerning their educational and financial development, are all illustrations. In a sense these boards are all engaged in propaganda work, the results of which it is difficult to evaluate.

tutions as they may decide are no longer useful.[30] These boards are not only taking a scientific attitude toward this problem, but they are studying their colleges to see what are needed and what are not needed, and are advocating, and in many cases effecting, the close of the superfluous institutions.[31]

6. COUNCIL OF CHURCH BOARDS OF EDUCATION.

There is one feature of this whole movement which seems to promise very great possibilities for good. That is the recently organized council of church boards of education. This council was organized in 1911, and has for its purpose a more intelligent cooperation among churches in the building and maintenance of church colleges.[32] Possibly it was the influence of the more powerful philanthropic agencies, together with the growing prestige of the great privately endowed and State universities, that brought the small church college to realize that its influence was beginning to wane.

This movement toward cooperation is one important outcome of the vigorous discussions of the place of the small college in American higher education. These boards knew many of the weak points in the church college situation and knew that duplication of effort was probably their greatest weakness.

At an informal conference of the secretaries of seven church boards of education, held in New York City, February 18, 1911, it was decided that a second conference should be held at which carefully prepared papers should be presented.

Such a conference was held and resulted in the following declaration of principles: (1) A large degree of cooperation between educational boards is practicable and desirable. " Through them we might secure a better geographical distribution of denominational colleges * * * a proper standardization of institutions," etc. (2) The denominations should offer loyal support to the public-school system. (3) The legitimacy and the absolute necessity of a certain number of denominational academies, occupying strategic positions in territory not fully occupied by the public high schools. (4) There should be a direct approach by the denominations to the problem of religious instruction at State university centers.[33]

The council took permanent form at the conclusion of this meeting and has since published annual reports of its work. Several practical steps toward cooperation between the boards have already been taken, and, though its place as a standardizing agency may remain advisory only, it is in that capacity that its influence as a philanthropic agency offers substantial promise.

SUMMARY AND CONCLUSIONS.

We may characterize this period in the growth of higher education in America as follows:

The question of State versus private endowment of higher education has been fought through and settled favorably to both methods; the church has continued its work of founding small colleges; several very large institutions (in a sense a new type) have been founded by the fortunes of single individuals and have not looked to the church for support; a number of large foundations,

---

[30] See Rep. Bd. of Educ. Meth. Epis. Ch., 1915, p. 23, for illustration.

[31] Black Hills College, 1903 ; Charles City College, University of the Pacific, and Fort Worth University, 1911 ; Mount Pleasant German College, 1908, are a few of the Methodist institutions that have been closed in this way.

[32] The constitution of the council is printed in the Second Annual Report of the Council of Church Boards of Education.

[33] See First An. Rep. of Council of Church Boards of Ed. in U. S. America.

the aim of which is research and general educational stimulus and supervision, have been created; and a new philosophy of education, which has found expression in the organization, administration, and management of our institutions of higher learning, has been worked out.

In opening up new territory to higher education during this period, the State has for the most part done the pioneering, thus reversing the custom of pre-Civil War days, when the church school led the way.

From a general view of the work of philanthropy in higher education, as gathered from the Reports of the United States Commissioner of Education, we have seen that philanthropy has gradually built up a vast fund for the permanent endowment of higher learning; that from this source, together with annual gifts, philanthropy is still bearing decidedly the larger part of the burden of higher education, though the State is assuming a relatively larger portion of this burden each year; and that tuition has covered practically the same percentage of the total annual cost from 1872 to the present. We have seen that, on an average, more than half of all gifts have gone to "permanent endowment and general purposes"; that there is a tendency in recent years for a larger proportion to go into the permanent funds; and that from one-eighth to one-half of the annual gifts have been for the development of the school plant. We have seen that in the seventies and eighties professorships and libraries fared well; that scholarships became increasingly important, and that the indigent never were quite forgotten; and, finally, that the percentage of all gifts that have been made without condition through the years has ranged from 4 to 26 per cent.

From other data we have seen that philanthropy has been almost solely responsible for the development of separate colleges for women, and for theological schools; that it has played a large part in the development of medical schools, and a small part in technical and law schools; and that private enterprise and the State have been almost entirely responsible for the development of schools of dentistry and pharmacy, while the State has been largely responsible for technical schools.

From data in the various annual publications from 1893 to 1915, inclusive, we have seen that education has received 43 per cent of all gifts of $5,000 or over in the United States; that charity is education's largest competitor, with 37 per cent; while "religious purposes" balances with museums and public improvements at approximately 9 per cent each, and libraries at 2 per cent. Roughly, and relatively speaking, we may say that during the first half of this period the amount of gifts for education made a slight gain, since which it has suffered a steady decline. Similarly religious purposes and museums have suffered a substantial though irregular decline from the start, while libraries have made a continuous decline from the first. These changes are in practically all cases only relative.

Among the old colonial colleges we have seen that the entire burden has fallen upon philanthropy and student fees, the States having offered no assistance whatever through this period. In spite of this, gifts have increased greatly. Conditional gifts have become somewhat more popular, but slightly the opposite is true with respect to gifts for permanent funds. Gifts to libraries and to indigent students have declined, while professorships have remained approximately as before.

In the colleges of the early national period we see the same rapid growth of funds from philanthropy as noted for the older institutions. In the colleges of this period the rapid growth of permanent funds is especially noticeable, and, further, the larger portion of these gifts are for the general fund. With this growth of general endowment have also prospered professorships, scholarships, and libraries.

As to the colleges of this period, no study was made of what we think of as the small church college. The work of this character is undoubtedly important, but there is little if anything new coming from it. The real contribution of the period is the group of large foundations. With one or two exceptions these are not church-fostered and not State-fostered institutions as all their ancestors have been. They encourage liberality in religion, they offer the most liberal scientific education for women, they encourage the use of museum and laboratory methods of teaching, and they foster research as a university function.

An examination of the financial history of this type of institution shows that in all cases they have been promptly taken over by the people and are now among the most important recipients of gifts in this country. Their rate of growth has been very great almost from the start, and all our evidence goes to show that these powerful financial corporations, planted in the midst of small colleges and accepted in some quarters with misgiving, have not only kept faith with earlier social, religious, and educational aims, but, in the readjustment of those aims to our rapidly expanding age, they have shown capacity proportionate to their great financial power, and what was to some a doubtful experiment is a success.

Through this period we have seen the continuation of the work of church boards of education, or religious education societies. These are rapidly increasing in numbers, there being a tendency for each church to have its own board. Their work has been conducted along two main lines. They have contributed scholarships either by gift or by loan, and they have made grants to colleges to meet either a general or some special need. Their chief aim has continued to be the development of a trained ministry, though the development of colleges in which all students will be kept in a proper religious atmosphere is scarcely secondary. The evidence presented shows that these societies have prospered. They are contributing direct assistance to many hundreds of students every year; they are making grants direct to colleges, grants which, though small, have often been directly responsible for larger gifts; they have in some measure exercised supervision over the founding of new schools, over curricula, and finance; and by their cooperation through the council of church boards of education they promise much more for the future.

Chapter V.
GREAT EDUCATIONAL FOUNDATIONS.

A NEW PHILANTHROPIC ENTERPRISE.

A type of philanthropic educational enterprise peculiar to the period just discussed is that of the large foundation whose purpose is not alone, nor even primarily, that of teaching but rather that of supplementing and assisting established institutions of education.

One can scarcely read the founding documents of these institutions without being struck first of all with the very wide scope of service which they have undertaken. The Peabody Fund promoted popular education in the South by cooperation with State and local officials. The Jeanes, the Slater, and the Phelps-Stokes Fund have been devoted to the problems of education for negroes. The Carnegie Foundation for the Advancement of Teaching has concerned itself with salaries, pensions, and insurance for college professors. The General Education Board has helped along several of these lines and paid much attention to educational investigations, and especially to a more substantial endowment of existing institutions. The Sage Foundation has contributed liberally by investigation, research, and publication.

These foundations, therefore, appear as a really new type of philanthropic enterprise in education, with church education boards as their only possible precedent, and though, as compared with the educational assets of some of our great cities, or with sums which numerous States are utilizing annually, or even with a few of our universities, they are not remarkably large, yet they are large enough to represent very great possibilities, and society can not afford to take them lightly. Can our country assimilate this new enterprise, is a question that might have been asked when Mr. Peabody and his successors began pouring out their millions in the development of this new *business*, the business of educational philanthropy.

The church college was antagonistic toward the State institutions of higher education when the latter began to grow rapidly into great universities, and they were also quite skeptical of the great privately endowed universities, lest they might be Godless schools. The State, the church, and the individual philanthropist were in a fairly real sense competitors in the field, and it was but natural that the old pioneer, the church college, should at first be jealous of what seemed to be its special prerogative. This rivalry has continued, but it has become increasingly friendly with passing years.

These new foundations, however, do not enter the field as rivals, but, instead, aim definitely to supplement and to cooperate with forces already at work. What work will they supplement and with whom will they cooperate are extremely practical questions which they must face, and also which the colleges and schools must face. Giving help to my competitor is in a sense the equivalent of doing harm to me. This was precisely the point of danger.

THE STATED PURPOSES OF THESE FOUNDATIONS.

First, then, what are the aims of these foundations, and what limitations are placed upon the funds which they are to manage? For these we must turn to their founding documents.

1. THE PEABODY EDUCATION FUND.

The Peabody Education Fund, the gift of George Peabody, of Massachusetts, was established in 1867, and amounted finally to $3,000,000. In a letter to 15 men whom he had chosen to act as his trustees, Mr. Peabody sets forth his plans and purposes, which were later embodied in the act of incorporation. He says:[1]

I give to you * * * the sum of one million dollars, to be by you and your successors held in trust, and the income thereof used and applied, in your discretion, for the promotion and encouragement of intellectual, moral, or industrial education among the young of the more destitute portions of the Southern and Southwestern States of our Union, my purpose being that the benefits intended shall be distributed among the entire population, without other distinction than their needs and the opportunities of usefulness to them.

In the following paragraph he empowers them to use 40 per cent of the principal sum within the next two years, then adds another million to the gift, grants the trustees power to incorporate, and further says:

In case two-thirds of the trustees shall at any time, after the lapse of 30 years, deem it expedient to close this trust, and of the funds which at that time shall be in the hands of yourselves and your successors to distribute not less than two-thirds among such educational and literary institutions, or for such educational purposes as they may determine, in the States for whose benefit the income is now appointed to be used. The remainder to be distributed by the trustees for educational or literary purposes wherever they may deem it expedient.

This letter, together with a later one in which he says, " I leave all the details of management to their (the trustees') own discretion," were embodied in the preamble to the charter later issued by the State of New York.

In June, 1869, Mr. Peabody addressed to the board a letter of appreciation for their service in carrying out his trust, in which he conveyed a gift of securities worth nearly a million and a half dollars.[2]

These letters certainly stand out as among the most remarkable documents in the history of educational philanthropy to this time. There were only the most general restrictions on the funds, and these were to end after 30 years, leaving the trustees almost entirely free to dispose of the entire fund. The best proof of their great distinction, as we shall see, lies in the fact that they have been the precedent for all similar subsequent foundations.

2. THE JOHN F. SLATER FUND.

The second of these foundations was the John F. Slater Fund for the Education of Freedmen, established on March 4, 1882, by a gift of $1,000,000. In a letter of date March 4, 1882, Mr. Slater invites 10 men to form a corporation for the administration of the fund, and in this letter he sets forth the purposes he wishes to achieve, together with the restrictions he places upon the gift. He names as the general object—

---

[1] See Proc. of Trustees of Peabody Educ. Fund, Vol. I, p. 1 ff.
[2] Peabody Educ. Fund, Proc., Vol. II, p. 142 ff.

the uplifting of the lately emancipated population of the Southern States, and their posterity, by conferring on them the blessings of Christian education.

He seeks not only—

for their own sake, but also for the safety of our common country [to provide them] with the means of such education as shall tend to make them good men and good citizens—education in which the instruction of the mind in the common branches of secular learning shall be associated with training in just notions of duty toward God and man, in the light of the Holy Scriptures.

The means to be used, he says, " I leave to the discretion of the corporation." He then suggests " the training of teachers from among the people " and " the encouragement of such institutions as are most effectually useful in promoting this training of teachers."

Further on he adds:

I purposely leave to the corporation the largest liberty of making such changes in the methods of applying the income of the fund as shall seem from time to time best adapted to accomplish the general object herein named.

He then, obviously drawing upon English experience, warns them against the possible evils of such endowments, and states that after 33 years they are to be free to dispose of the capital of the fund—

to the establishment of foundations subsidiary to these already existing institutions of higher education, in such wise as to make the educational advantages of such institutions more freely accessible to poor students of the colored race.

Finally, he urges the avoidance of any partisan, sectional, or sectarian bias in the use of the gift, and closes with reference to the success of the Peabody Education Fund as having encouraged him to establish this foundation.[3]

This letter was embodied in the charter issued by New York State in April, 1882. In all the fundamentals these documents are a fair copy of the charter and instruments of gift in the case of the Peabody Education Fund.

3. THE CARNEGIE INSTITUTION.

The third of these foundations to take form was the Carnegie Institution of Washington. The trust deed by which it was established is of date January 28, 1902, and transfers to the trustees securities worth $10,000,000. (This sum has since been more than doubled.) In this instrument of gift[4] Mr. Carnegie declares it to be his purpose to found in Washington an institution which, with the corporation of other institutions—

shall in the broadest and most liberal manner encourage investigation, research, and discovery—show the application of knowledge to the improvement of mankind, provide such buildings, laboratories, books, and apparatus as may be needed; and afford instruction of an advanced character to students properly qualified to profit thereby.

It aims, he says:

1. To promote original research.
2. To discover the exceptional man in every department of study * * * and enable him to make the work for which he seems specially designed his life work.
3. To increase facilities for higher education.
4. To increase the efficiency of the universities and other institutions of learning [both by adding to their facilities and by aiding teachers in experimental studies].
5. To enable such students as may find Washington the best point for their special studies to enjoy the advantages of the museums [and other numerous institutions].

---

[3] For a copy of this letter and the charter see Proceedings of the John F. Slater Fund for the Education of Freedmen, 1883, p. 21 ff.

[4] See Carnegie Institution of Washington, Year Book No. 1, 1902.

6. To insure the prompt publication and distribution of the results of scientific investigation.

Finally:

The trustees shall have power, by a majority of two-thirds of their number, to modify the conditions and regulations under which the funds may be dispensed, so as to secure that these shall always be applied in the manner best adapted to the advanced conditions of the times; provided always that any modifications shall be in accordance with the purposes of the donor, as expressed in the trust.

4. THE GENERAL EDUCATION BOARD.

Following this in 1903 the General Education Board was established by John D. Rockefeller. His preliminary gift in 1902 of $1,000,000 was followed in 1905 by a gift of $10,000,000, and this by a third gift of $32,000,000 in 1907, and a fourth, of $10,000,000, in 1909.

In the act of incorporation Mr. Rockefeller states the purposes of the foundation as follows:

SEC. 2. That the object of the said corporation shall be the promotion of education within the United States of America, without distinction of race, sex, or creed.

SEC. 3. That for the promotion of such object the said corporation shall have power to build, improve, enlarge, or equip, or to aid others to build, improve, enlarge, or equip, buildings for elementary or primary schools, industrial schools, technical schools, normal schools, training schools for teachers, or schools of any grade, or for higher institutions of learning, or, in connection therewith, libraries, workshops, gardens, kitchens, or other educational accessories; to establish, maintain, or endow, or aid others to establish, maintain, or endow, elementary or primary schools, industrial schools, technical schools, normal schools, training schools for teachers, or schools of any grade, or higher institutions of learning; to employ or aid others to employ teachers and lecturers; to aid, cooperate with, or endow associations or other corporations engaged in educational work within the United States of America, or to donate to any such association or corporation any property or moneys which shall at any time be held by the said corporation hereby constituted; to collect educational statistics and information, and to publish and distribute documents and reports containing the same, and in general to do and perform all things necessary or convenient for the promotion of the object of the corporation.

In a letter from John D. Rockefeller, jr., of date March 2, 1902, the conditions which are to control the uses to which the money may be put are set forth. These limitations were subsequently changed. Originally, however, referring to the above statement of purpose, the letter says:

Upon this understanding my father hereby pledges to the board the sum of one million dollars ($1,000,000) to be expended at its discretion during a period of 10 years, and will make payments under such pledges from time to time as requested by the board or its executive committee through its duly authorized officers.

The second gift is announced in a letter from Mr. F. T. Gates, which states the following conditions:

The principal to be held in perpetuity as a foundation for education, the income above expenses of administration to be distributed to, or used for the benefit of, such institutions of learning, at such times, in such amounts, for such purposes and under such conditions, or employed in such other ways, as the board may deem best adapted to promote a comprehensive system of higher education in the United States.

The third gift was presented through a letter from Mr. Rockefeller, jr., and the conditions controlling the uses of the money are:

---

[5] See The General Education Board, An Account of Its Activities, 1902–1914, p. 212 ff.
[6] Ibid., p. 213.

One-third to be added to the permanent endowment of the board, two-thirds to be applied to such specific objects within the corporate purposes of the board as either he or I may from time to time direct, any remainder, not so designated at the death of the survivor, to be added to the permanent endowment of the board.

Concerning the fourth gift Mr. Rockefeller says, through a letter from his son addressed to the board, that the gift is to be added to the permanent endowment of the board. Then follow these qualifications:

He, however, authorizes and empowers you and your successors, whenever in your discretion it shall seem wise, to distribute the principal or any part thereof, provided the same shall be authorized by a resolution passed by the affirmative vote of two-thirds of all those who shall at the time be members of your board at a special meeting held on not less than 30 days' notice given in writing, which shall state that the meeting is called for the purpose of considering a resolution to authorize the distribution of the whole or some part of the principal of said fund. Upon the adoption of such resolution in the manner above described, you and your successors shall be and are hereby released from the obligation thereafter to hold in perpetuity or as endowment such portion of the principal of such fund as may have been authorized to be distributed by such resolution.

This would seem to give the board very wide powers and to leave to the donor very little control aside from a part of the third gift specially reserved. Yet Mr. Rockefeller seems not to have been fully satisfied, for on June 29, 1909, he addressed a letter to the board saying:

GENTLEMEN: I have heretofore from time to time given to your board certain property, the principal of which was to be held in perpetuity, or as endowment. I now authorize and empower you and your successors, whenever in your discretion it shall seem wise, to distribute the principal or any part thereof, provided the same shall be authorized by a resolution passed by the affirmative vote of two-thirds of all those who shall at the time be members of your board, at a special meeting held on not less than 30 days' notice given in writing, which shall state that the meeting is called for the purpose of considering a resolution to authorize the distribution of the whole, or some part of the principal of said funds. Upon the adoption of such resolution in the manner above prescribed, you and your successors shall be, and are hereby, released from the obligation thereafter to hold in perpetuity or as endowment such portion of the principal of such funds as may have been authorized to be distributed by such resolution.

It would be hard to think of a point at which this board could be given wider freedom in the exercise of its jurisdiction over these funds than is here granted by the founder.

5. THE CARNEGIE FOUNDATION.

The fifth of these foundations, the Carnegie Foundation for the Advancement of Teaching, had its origin in a letter, of date April 16, 1905, in which Mr. Carnegie set forth to a group of 25 men whom he had chosen to act as his trustees the plan of his foundation.[7] In all he has placed $16,250,000 in the hands of this board. The plan is clearly stated in the charter which was obtained in March, 1906. Here the object is declared to be:

To provide retiring pensions, without regard to race, sex, creed, or color, for the teachers of universities, colleges, and technical schools in the United States, the Dominion of Canada, and Newfoundland, who, by reason of long and meritorious service, or by reason of old age, disability, or other sufficient reason, shall be deemed entitled to the assistance and aid of this corporation, on such terms and conditions, however, as such corporation may from time to time approve and adopt.

---

[7] Quoted in full in the first annual report of the president and treasurer of the Carnegie Foundation for the Advancement of Teaching.

Then follows the limitation that those connected with any institution which is controlled by a sect or which imposes any theological test as a condition of entrance into or connection therewith are excluded.

In general, to do and perform all things necessary to encourage, uphold, and dignify the profession of the teacher and the cause of higher education * * *, and to promote the object of the foundation, with full power, however, to the trustee hereinafter appointed and their successors, from time to time to modify the conditions and regulations under which the work shall be carried on, so as to secure the application of the funds in the manner best adapted to the conditions of the times; [and provided that by two-thirds vote the trustees may] enlarge or vary the purposes herein set forth, provided that the objects of the corporation shall at all times be among the foregoing and kindred thereto.[8]

6. THE RUSSELL SAGE FOUNDATION.

In April, 1907, the sixth of these, the Russel Sage Foundation, was chartered by the State of New York. The charter states the purpose of the corporation to be that of—

Receiving and maintaining a fund or funds and applying the income thereof to the improvement of social and living conditions in the United States of America. It shall be within the purposes of said corporation to use any means to that end which from time to time shall seem expedient to its members or trustees, including research, publication, education, the establishment and maintenance of charitable or benevolent activities and institutions, and the aid of any such activities, agencies, or institutions already established.

In her letter of gift, of date April 19, 1907, Mrs. Sage says: " I do not wish to enlarge or limit the powers given to the foundation by its act of incorporation,"[9] but adds that it seems wise to express certain desires to which she would wish the trustees to conform. Then follows several suggestions relative to local and national use of the funds, types of investments, etc., which in the writer's judgment tend to enlarge the freedom which most men serving as trustees would otherwise have been inclined to exercise over the funds under the charter.

7. THE PHELPS-STOKES FUND.

The seventh of these foundations was the Phelps-Stokes Fund of nearly $1,000,000, which was established by the bequest of Caroline Phelps Stokes, who made her will in 1893 and died in 1909. The foundation was chartered in 1911. In her will Miss Stokes says: " I direct that all my residuary estate * * * shall be given by my executors to the following persons " (here she names the trustees she has chosen, and adds) :

To invest and keep invested by them and their successors, the interest and net income of such fund to be used by them and their successors for the erection or improvement of tenement-house dwellings in New York City for the poor families of New York City and for educational purposes in the education of the negroes both in Africa and the United States, North American Indians, and needy and deserving white students, through industrial schools of kinds similar to that at Northfield, Mass., in which Mr. Dwight L. Moody is interested, or to the Peet Industrial School at Asheville, N. C., the foundation of scholarships and the erection or endowment of school buildings * * *. I hereby give said trustees and their successors full power of sale, public or private, in their discretion, upon such terms as they think best respecting any part of said trust fund in the course of the due execution of such trust.[10]

---

[8] "Act of Incorporation, By-Laws, Rules for Granting of Retiring Allowances," N. Y., 1906.

[9] For copies of this letter and of the charter the writer is indebted to Dr. John M. Glenn, director of the foundation.

[10] From Phelps-Stokes Fund—Act of Incorporation, By-Laws, and Other Documents.

The charter, in defining the purpose of the foundation, uses much of this same language and in addition the following:

It shall be within the purpose of said corporation to use any means to such ends * * *, including research, publication, the establishment and maintenance of charitable or benevolent activities, agencies, and institutions, and the aid of any such activities, agencies, or institutions already established.[11]

This fund stands as a permanent endowment, but with such very general conditions placed upon its use that it is virtually as free as it could be made.

8. THE ROCKEFELLER FOUNDATION.

The latest foundation of just this type to be established is that of the Rockefeller Foundation, incorporated in April, 1913. The purpose of the corporation is that—

of receiving and maintaining a fund or funds, and applying the income and principal thereof, to promote the well-being of mankind throughout the world.

Its means are to be—

research, publication, the establishment and maintenance of charitable, benevolent, religious, missionary, and public educational activities, agencies, and institutions, and the aid of any such activities, agencies, and institutions already established, and any other means and agencies which from time to time shall seem expedient to its members or trustees.[12]

9. THE CLEVELAND FOUNDATION.

There is one other type of foundation that is of very recent origin, but which is rapidly becoming popular, and shows promise of becoming very extensive and powerful in the near future. The chief work of this corporation is not education, but since educational service is within its powers it deserves mention here. The Cleveland Foundation, organized in January, 1914, was the first of this type, since followed by the Chicago Community Trust, the Houston Foundation, the Los Angeles Community Foundation, the St. Louis Community Trust, the Spokane Foundation, and other foundations of similar character at Milwaukee, Boston, Indianapolis, Ind., Attleboro, Mass., Minneapolis, Detroit, and Seattle. The Cleveland Foundation was formed by resolution of the board of directors of the Cleveland Trust Co., in which the company agreed to act as trustee of property given and devised for charitable purposes, all property to be administered as a single trust. The income of this foundation is administered by a committee appointed partly by the trustee company and partly by the mayor, the judge of the probate court, and the Federal district judge. The principal is managed by the trustee company.

The resolution creating the trust sets forth the object of the foundation as follows:[13]

From the time the donor or testator provides that income shall be available for use of such foundation, such income less proper charges and expenses shall be annually devoted perpetually to charitable purposes, unless principal is distributed as hereinafter provided. Without limiting in any way the charitable purposes for which such income may be used, it shall be available for assisting charitable and educational institutions, whether supported by private donations or public taxation, for promoting education, scientific research, for care of the sick, aged, or helpless, to improve living conditions, or to provide recreation for all classes, and for such other charitable purposes as will best make for the mental, moral, and physical improvement of the

---

[11] Ibid., p. 5 ff.
[12] An Act to Incorporate The Rockefeller Foundation, in Ann. Rep.
[13] From " The Cleveland Foundation a Community Trust," The Cleveland Trust Co., 1914.

inhabitants of the city of Cleveland, as now or hereafter constituted, regardless of race, color, or creed, according to the discretion of a majority in number of a committee to be constituted as hereinafter provided.

It is further provided that if contributors to the foundation, in their instruments of gift, place limitations as to the final disposition of the principal, or as to the uses to which its income may be put, or as to what members of the trust company shall exercise control over the disposition of principal or interest, then—

The trustee shall respect and be governed by the wishes as so expressed, but only in so far as the purposes indicated shall seem to the trustee, under conditions as they may hereafter exist, wise and most widely beneficial, absolute discretion being vested in a majority of the then members of the board of directors of the Cleveland Trust Co. to determine with respect thereto.

When by the exercise of this power funds are diverted from the purposes indicated by their respective donors, such funds "shall be used and distributed for the general purposes of the foundation."

The foundation is to provide a committee for distributing its funds, the committee to be made up of—

Residents of Cleveland, men or women interested in welfare work, possessing a knowledge of the civic, educational, physical, and moral needs of the community, preferably but one, and in no event to exceed two members of said committee to belong to the same religious sect or denomination, those holding or seeking political office to be disqualified from serving.

Two members of the committee are to be appointed by the Cleveland Trust Co., one by the mayor, one by the senior or presiding judge of the court which settles estates in Cuyahoga County, and one by the senior or presiding judge of the United States District Court for the Northern District of Ohio. This committee is to be provided with a paid secretary, but otherwise to receive expenses only.

There are other interesting features of this resolution. For instance, when the income of any trust is available for use by the foundation—

All or any portion of the property belonging to such trust may be listed for taxation, regardless of any statute exempting all or any part thereof by reason of its application to charitable purposes, if a majority of the board of directors of the Cleveland Trust Co. shall so direct.

And more important still is the provision that—

With the approval of two-thirds of the entire board of directors of the Cleveland Trust Co., given at a meeting called specifically for that purpose, all or any part of the principal constituting the trust estate may be used for any purpose within the scope of the foundation, which may have the approval of four members of said committee, providing that not to exceed 20 per cent of the entire amount held as principal shall be disbursed during a period of five consecutive years.

Careful provision is made for an annual audit of all accounts, and full control of funds and properties is vested in the trustees of the foundation.

This is clearly a new method of handling philanthropy. In a sense it is an ordinary commission business with unusually good security for its patrons. From the standpoint of the bank it promises fair though not lucrative profit. It is so designed as to keep its business exclusively for the city of Cleveland, so that fortunes accumulated there by the few eventually may be turned back to the community in the form of some kind of public service. Looked at from another angle, it is a real community enterprise which ought to develop civic pride as well as contribute to the solution of local social and educational problems. It makes philanthropy possible for small as well as large fortunes, and so tends to popularize giving. The large fund that promises to accumulate is always adaptable to whatever changes the future may bring. It is undoubtedly an interesting and important business and social experiment by which education may hope to profit.

This places before us in fairly complete form the aims and purposes of this rather new type of educational enterprise. The Anna T. Jeanes Foundation is very similar in character but deals with elementary education exclusively. Similarly there are numerous other foundations engaged in charitable, library, or research work whose founding instruments embody the same fundamental principles common to those here quoted and, viewed from the standpoint of the evolution of a theory of endowments, belong in the same class.

To state these principles in brief we may say, first of all, that the " purpose " is in every case set forth in the most general terms and in brief and simple language; second, that the means for carrying out this purpose is left almost entirely to the trustees of the foundation; third, that the means, and to an extent in some cases even the purpose, is modifiable at the will of the trustees; and fourth, that there is no sectional, racial, denominational, political, or ecclesiastical control. In most cases the capital fund is to remain permanently intact, but in some cases the entire income and capital may be used and the trust terminated. The Peabody Education Fund illustrates how this latter plan has already operated in full. The possible scope of activities is practically national for all, and international for some, the boards of trustees are self-perpetuating, and they receive no pay for their services.

This means that there is every possibility for keeping these large sums of money, now amounting to more than $300,000,000, constantly in touch with the real educational needs of the country, and in these charters there seems no possibility that it will ever be necessary for any one of these foundations to continue to do any particular thing in any particular way—as, for instance, to maintain " enough faggots to burn a heretic "—in order to control the available funds to some entirely desirable and profitable end.

THE OPERATIONS OF THESE FOUNDATIONS.

The real test of these liberal provisions could come only when educational philanthropy as a business began actually to cope with the educational, social, and economic forces in the midst of which it sought a place of responsibility.

A half century of activity has passed since the first of these foundations began its work. During the first 15 years of this period the Peabody Fund stood alone. Then came the Slater Fund, after which 20 years passed before the next, the Carnegie Institution at Washington, was established. This foundation by Mr. Carnegie seemed to initiate a new era in respect both to the number and size of these endowments.

1. THE PEABODY EDUCATION FUND.

When the Peabody Education Fund began its work there were few public-school systems of consequence in the South, either city or State. With this fund Dr. Barnas Sears attacked this problem directly, and by 1875 had so popularized the idea that cities and States were taking over the schools which the fund had established. The next move was for the training of teachers for these schools. Arrangements were made to turn the University of Nashville to this purpose, its new name to be Peabody Normal College. This was done in 1875, and a large number of scholarships were established. Later, attention was turned to summer normals, to teachers' institutes, and gradually to the development of normal schools in each of the States.

Doctor Curry, who succeeded Doctor Sears, carried forward the development of normal schools, but in his work began to condition his gifts upon the State's making appropriations to go with them. Doctor Curry was repeatedly before State legislatures, defending the claims of public education; and when, in 1898, it was proposed to make final division of the fund by endowing one or more institutions, practically every Southern State protested against it. This disposition of the fund was finally made in 1913–14, with the endowment of the George Peabody College for Teachers.

During the years 1868 to 1914 the foundation gave away $3,650,-556 to the following: [a]

1. City public schools	$1,148,183
2. Normal schools	759,122
3. Teachers' institutes	382,755
4. George Peabody College	550,381
5. Scholarships	580,665
6. Educational journals	8,300
7. Summer schools	32,500
8. Rural public schools	37,800
9. State supervision of rural schools	77,950
10. Educational campaigns	13,500
11. County supervision of teaching	15,000
12. Miscellaneous	44,400

The final distribution of the fund, with its accrued income, was as follows:

George Peabody College for Teachers	1,500,000
University of Virginia	40,000
University of North Carolina	40,000
University of Georgia	40,000
University of Alabama	40,000
University of Florida	40,000
University of Missisippi	40,000
Louisiana State University	40,000
University of Arkansas	40,000
University of Kentucky	40,000
Johns Hopkins University	6,000
University of South Carolina	6,000
University of Missouri	6,000
University of Texas	6,000
Winthrop Normal College	90,000
John F. Slater Fund (education of negroes), estimated at	350,000

Table 36 will give some slight notion of the service rendered by the fund, if we keep in mind, first, that no one of the 11 States receiving aid from the fund in 1871 was itself contributing as much as $800,000 for common schools, and that at least 2 of these States spent less than $200,000 each; [14] and second, that these sums were so placed by the foundation as to stimulate interest in the idea of public schools.

The difficulty of the task which this foundation has performed must not be overlooked. It is specially noteworthy that from the beginning its agents worked in the open, frankly as a big propaganda enterprise. Both by addresses and by publications the people were kept informed as to just what the foundation sought to do.

---

[a] Proc. Peabody Educ. Fund, Vol. VI, p. 634 ff.
[14] See Rep. of U. S. Commis. of Educ., 1871.

TABLE 36.—*Distribution of the gifts of the Peabody Education Fund, 1868-1910, in 9 to 12 Southern States.*[1]

Dates.	To States.	To Normal College, Nashville.	Scholarships in Normal College, Nashville.	Total grants.	Dates.	To States.	To Normal College, Nashville.	Scholarships in Normal College, Nashville.	Total grants.
1868	$35,400			$35,400	1890	$43,376	$28,250	$21,474	$93,100
1869	90,000			90,000	1891	49,524	14,350	23,726	87,600
1870	90,500			90,500	1892	54,800	14,000	23,600	92,400
1871	100,000			100,000	1893	47,500	13,200	26,450	87,150
1872	130,000			130,000	1894	39,688	11,600	25,188	76,388
1873	136,850			136,850	1895	34,551	20,300	35,131	89,981
1874	134,600			134,600	1896	49,019	6,212	19,008	74,239
1875	98,000	$3,000		101,000	1897	45,100	9,900	23,567	60,567
1876	73,300	3,000		76,300	1898	45,700	14,600	24,498	84,798
1877	78,850	15,000	$1,900	95,750	1899	45,114	14,750	24,709	84,573
1878	57,600	5,000	1,900	64,500	1900	43,604	15,100	25,351	84,055
1879	64,500	11,000	12,300	87,800	1901	41,300	14,600	24,329	80,229
1880	42,900	13,000	10,400	66,350	1902	41,100	14,600	24,180	79,880
1881	34,125	4,000	25,975	64,100	1903	36,673	14,600	24,127	75,400
1882	49,350	8,000	16,150	73,509	1904	38,400	16,600	25,000	80,000
1883	46,925	9,500	20,700	77,125	1905	52,500	25,500		78,000
1884	31,600	9,900	21,200	62,700	1906	54,500	37,500		92,000
1885	31,995	10,100	20,970	63,065	1907	35,000	45,000		80,000
1886	46,000	10,000	18,500	74,500	1908				80,000
1887	31,600	10,500	24,300	66,400	1909				69,000
1888	23,600	7,800	17,800	49,200	1910				36,500
1889	39,750	10,950	26,450	77,150					

[1] Compiled from Rept. of U. S. Commis. Educ. for 1903 and from An. Proc. of Peabody Educ. Fund.

It is easy to imagine that society might have been much more skeptical of such an agency than it seems to have been. The growth of public-school systems and of normal and industrial schools in the South is evidence enough that the fund has been greatly useful, and its success stands as a monument to the capacity of the southern people to furnish the type of public opinion necessary to direct such a philanthropic force into useful channels. In this, however, public opinion would have failed had not its founder left it free to meet the changing conditions which came with the passing years. This, as our first exper'ment, must be pronounced a decided success and it must stand as an excellent precedent both for the future public and for the future philanthropist.

2. THE JOHN F. SLATER FUND.

The John F. Slater Fund was handled on so nearly the same lines, to so nearly the same ends, in the same territory, and for many years by the same agent as was the Peabody Education Fund that detailed examination of its work would add little if anything new to this discussion.

3. THE CARNEGIE INSTITUTION OF WASHINGTON, D. C.

The work of the Carnegie Institution of Washington is difficult to describe in terms that will show what its contribution has really been.[15] In explaining the policy for the future, it is made clear that " grounds already occupied will be avoided," [16] and that the institution considers that systematic education in universities, colleges, professional schools, and schools of technology, and the assistance of meritorious students in the early stages of their studies are already provided for and are therefore outside the scope of the foundation.

[15] For brief description and historical development of the institution, see The Carnegie Institution of Washington—Scope and Organization, Fourth issue, Feb. 4, 1915, by the institution; also Seven Great Foundations, by Leonard P. Ayres; also retrospective review of, in the Eleventh Year Book of the institution.

[16] Carnegie Institution of Washington, Year Book, No. 1, 1902, p. xli.

From the outset the institution has directed its work along four lines as follows: Large research projects covering a series of years and managed by a corps of investigators; small research projects, usually directed by single individuals and for a brief period; tentative investigations by young men or women of aptitude for research; and publication of the results of its own studies and of meritorious work which would not otherwise be readily published. The order of development of its larger departments of research is worthy of notice here. They were as follows:

Department of Experimental Evolution	December, 1903
Department of Marine Biology	December, 1903
Department of Historical Research	December, 1903
Department of Economics and Sociology [17]	January, 1904
Department of Terrestrial Magnetism	April, 1904
Solar Observatory	December, 1904
Geographical Laboratory	December, 1905
Department of Botanical Research	December, 1905
Nutrition Laboratory	December, 1906
Department of Meridian Astronomy	March, 1907
Department of Embryology	December, 1914

To these larger fields of operation must be added special researches in almost every possible field, and even a casual reading of the annual reports of the institution shows that the division of administration has itself served as a research laboratory of no mean proportions.[18]

From the nature of its work it is evident that the relations of the institution to universities and to learned societies would have to be guarded. This the institution has tried to do by keeping out of occupied fields and by dealing with individuals concerned with specific pieces of research. The outside world has apparently raised little question as to the privileges and responsibilities of this institution, but with the society of scholars it has numerous conflicts, if the brief hints in the reports of the president are indicative of the content of his letter files.[19] It is in the face of this type of public opinion that this institution will continue to adjust itself to its proper place in society, and also to work out a fundamental theory of administration for this new type of educational enterprise, which, together with its help in popularizing scientific method and the use of the results of research, will constitute no small part of its total contribution.

Any study of the finances, or of the amount of work done, or of the number of studies published, or of the number of houses, laboratories, observatories, and ships owned and utilized by the institution can add but little to any attempt to evaluate this type of philanthropic enterprise. The following table showing the annual appropriations and the volume and page extent of its published researches is of some value, however, when we consider that these sums have been spent in fields that could not have been so fully explored if the several hundred investigators employed had been compelled to meet the usual demands made upon the time of a university professor:

[17] Discontinued as a department of the institution in 1916.
[18] See especially the president's study of definitions of " humanities " in the 16th Year Book, 1917, p. 16 ff.
[19] See especially the 14th Year Book of the institution.

TABLE 37.—*Distribution of appropriations made by the Carnegie Institution of Washington, 1902–1917.*[1]

Fiscal years.	Investments in bonds.	Large projects.	Minor projects and special associates and assistants.	Publications.	Administration.	Total.	Volumes published.	
							Number.	Pages.
1902.........			$4,500		$27,513	$32,013	3	46
1903.........	$100,475		137,564	$938	43,627	282,605	3	1,667
1904.........	196,159	$49,848	217,383	11,590	36,967	511,949	11	2,877
1905.........	51,937	269,940	149,843	21,822	37,208	530,753	21	5,228
1906.........	63,015	381,972	93,176	42,431	42,621	623,216	19	4,454
1907.........	2,000	500,548	90,176	63,804	46,005	702,534	38	9,712
1908.........	68,209	448,404	61,282	49,991	48,274	676,163	28	7,328
1909.........	116,756	495,021	70,813	41,577	45,292	769,460	19	4,907
1910.........	57,889	437,941	73,464	49,067	44,011	662,373	29	8,105
1911.........	51,921	463,609	63,048	37,580	45,455	661,616	30	6,732
1912.........	436,276	519,673	103,241	44,054	43,791	1,147,047	23	6,025
1913.........	666,428	698,337	110,083	53,171	43,552	1,571,572	29	9,357
1914.........	861,915	817,894	107,456	44,670	44,159	1,876,096	23	6,912
1915.........	206,203	770,488	109,569	46,698	48,224	1,181,183	23	6,152
1916.........	473,702	638,281	99,401	73,733	49,454	1,334,572	35	11,908
1917.........	505,473	695,813	97,526	62,884	48,776	1,410,464	21	7,155
Total..	3,858,363	7,187,775	1,588,531	644,017	694,936	13,973,614	335	88,565

[1] From 16th Yearbook, p. 29. Cents omitted.

Several points about these figures are of interest. During the 16 years recorded in the table the unused funds have accumulated, furnishing a 'substantial reserve fund for special needs. Aside from the first three years from 45 to 60 per cent of the appropriations have been for large department projects; from 5 to 12 per cent have been for the smaller investigations, the tendency being to give rather less to this item; from 2 to 10 per cent have been for publications, also with a tendency to decrease. During the first year only a small appropriation was made, approximately 86 per cent of all going for administration. During the second year only about 15 per cent went for administration, and for the remaining years the amount has been 7 per cent or less, declining to only 3 or 4 per cent in the six years ending in 1917.

There are no figures with which these properly can be compared, but they stand as the experience of 16 years spent in developing an entirely new type of institution. To the universities of the country it has not only furnished a great stimulus to research, but it has also given much direct assistance by financing important pieces of investigation and by publishing finished pieces of research.

4. THE GENERAL EDUCATION BOARD.

Mr. Rockefeller referred to the General Education Board as "an organization formed for the purpose of working out, in an orderly and rather scientific way, the problem of helping to stimulate and improve education in all parts of the country." [20]

The experience of the Peabody Fund in cooperating with State, county, and city officials was at hand and had been thoroughly studied.[21] Just how to cooperate with other forces, public and private, was the first specific problem of the General Education Board.

---

[20] Rockefeller, John D. The Benevolent Trust, the Cooperative Principle in Giving. The Worlds Work, vol. 17, Jan., 1909.

[21] See The General Education Board, 1902–1914, p. 13 ff.

Leaving aside the question of how this was accomplished in the matter of farm demonstration work and in elementary and secondary education in the South, we are concerned here with the board's work in the field of higher education.

One of the terms of Mr. Rockefeller's second gift to the board was that assistance should be given to—

such institutions of learning as the board may deem best adapted to promote a comprehensive system of higher education in the United States.

The fact was we had no system of higher education, and this corporation proposed to do what it could toward that most laudable end. Schools had been developed by the church, the State, and private enterprise, each working with but little reference to the other, denominational competition and politics often resulting in quite the opposite of system.

If this new board was to work toward a " system of higher education," then it must inevitably clash with these already conflicting enterprises, or somehow effect a coordination of their various forces. Some definite policy, therefore, had to be decided upon. Two principles of procedure were laid down, as follows: The board neither possessed nor desired any authority, and would not seek directly or indirectly to bias the action of any college or university; in making an appropriation the board would in no way interfere with the internal management of an institution nor incur any responsibility for its conduct.

When and where and how to apply these principles was the practical task. In 1916–17 the board reported that in all it had assisted 112 colleges and universities in 32 States. During the year 1916–17 the board contributed a total of $1,185,000 toward a total of $5,300,000 in gifts to 9 colleges. When we consider that for this same year Harvard received from gifts as much as $1,934,947, Columbia $1,390,594, and Chicago $3,181,543 we can see that the board had to find some basis for making choice among its many possible beneficiaries.

Making this choice was precisely what Mr. Rockefeller wanted to have done scientifically. To do it was to demonstrate that philanthropy could be made a successful business enterprise. Accordingly, extensive studies of the question were undertaken, and to date almost the entire college field has been surveyed with respect to certain main issues, and those colleges to which contributions have been made have been studied minutely. The result is a mine of important and systematically organized information about our higher institutions of learning that had not hitherto been available. These studies can not be adequately described, nor their value satisfactorily explained in few words.[22] As a method of giving they stand as a permanent contribution of value. They have meant that fact rather than sentiment has guided the board from the start.

The board has made a somewhat modest statement [23] of certain clearly evident improvements that have resulted from their strict adherence to this method of giving, as follows:

First, is that of more careful accounting systems.

Second, it has necessitated a clarification of certain terms, such as " capital," " endowment," " scientific equipment," etc., the very loose usage of which had

---

[22] There is plenty of evidence on file in the board rooms to show that many benefactors are utilizing these studies in placing their gifts.

[23] The General Education Board, 1902–1914, p. 149 ff.

previously made it impossible to compare financial statistics of different institutions.

Third, it has put an end to the practice, rather common among colleges, of using the principal of endowment funds on the assumption that the sum so taken was a loan and would later be replaced.

Fourth, it has brought about a distinction in practice between the educational budget of a college and its various business activities, such as the running of a boarding hall.

Fifth, it has resulted in a sort of departmental accounting, which has helped not only to distinguish costs in college from costs in preparatory departments but has tended to help even in defining what work is of college and what is of academy grade.

This board has operated on one other principle that deserves mention, viz, that any college that can not raise some money from its own natural clientele is scarcely to be thought of as very necessary to the community. Accordingly, it has been the practice of the board to contribute a sum toward a much larger total which the college must raise. Mr. Rockefeller said that—

to give to institutions that ought to be supported by others is not the best philanthropy. Such giving only serves to dry up the natural springs of charity.[24]

The application of this principle has not only brought large gifts to education that probably would never have been given otherwise, but it has helped toward placing the responsibility for the growth of these colleges where it belongs—upon large numbers of interested friends.

Another condition from which the board varies but rarely is that the entire gift, of which their own forms a part, shall be preserved inviolate for the permanent endowment of the institution. This recognizes the need for general, as opposed to special, endowment funds. Another provision is that no part of the board's gift can ever be used for theological instruction.

During the last few years the board has entered upon two other lines of work—that of financing and directing educational investigations and that of putting clinical instruction in the medical schools of John Hopkins, Yale, and Washington Universities upon a full-time basis. This latter was not an untried experiment, but it was certainly in an early experimental stage in this country.

The field of educational investigation was not new, but the demand for such work was by no means fully met by other agencies. The survey of the Maryland State school system; the more recent report of a survey of the schools of Gary, Ind.; and the experimental work on reading and writing scales at Chicago University and with gifted pupils at Illinois University; as well as the experimental school at Teachers College, Columbia University, are some of the results so far obtained in this field, all of which give large promise.

The following table will give at most an inadequate notion of the work that has thus far been accomplished by the foundation:

---

[24] In World's Work, above cited.

TABLE 38.—*Total appropriations of the General Education Board from its foundation in 1902 to June 30, 1918.*[1]

(The Rockefeller Fund.)

	Amount appropriated.	Amount paid.	Amount unpaid.
For whites:			
Universities and colleges for endowment	$13,873,704	$10,278,617	$3,595,087
Colleges and schools for current expenses	174,991	174,991	....
Medical schools for endowment	5,603,774	2,770,874	2,832,900
Professors of secondary education	379,339	343,089	36,250
Rural school agents	230,476	172,206	58,270
Lincoln school	219,250	104,250	115,000
Consolidated rural schools	21,500	11,500	10,000
Southern education board	97,126	97,126	....
	20,600,162	13,952,654	6,647,507
For negroes:			
Colleges and schools for current expenses and buildings ...	1,249,775	1,141,282	108,492
Medical schools for current expenses	15,000	15,000	....
Rural school agents	208,120	153,066	50,054
Summer schools	19,891	11,839	8,052
County training schools	49,797	28,604	21,193
Home-makers' Clubs	90,989	58,768	32,220
Expenses of special students at Hampton and Tuskegee	17,865	3,615	14,250
Scholarships	5,000	300	4,700
Negro Rural School Fund	59,400	41,400	18,000
John F. Slater Fund	3,000	....	3,000
	1,718,839	1,458,876	259,962
Agricultural work (white and negro):			
Southern agricultural demonstration work	716,077	716,077	....
Girls' canning and poultry work in the South	113,751	113,751	....
Maine agricultural demonstration work	120,876	95,876	25,000
New Hampshire agricultural demonstration work	64,093	48,093	16,000
Rural organization service	36,646	36,646	....
	1,051,446	1,010,466	41,000
Miscellaneous (white and negro):			
Educational investigation and research	158,354	122,988	35,366
General survey of educational conditions and needs in North Carolina	5,000	....	5,000
Cost-accounting system for Gary	1,025	1,025	....
Expenses rural school agents at Harvard summer school	7,000	....	7,000
Model county organization	28,150	20,500	7,650
Conferences	19,438	19,438	....
Supplemental fund	7,772	7,772	....
	226,741	171,724	55,016
Income on hand June 30, 1918	....	....	8,035,988
Unpaid appropriations as above	....	....	7,903,486
Unappropriated income June 30, 1918	....	....	1,032,501

[1] See An. Rept., Gen. Educ. Bd., 1917–18, pp. 84–85. Cents omitted.

In addition to the foregoing the sum of $110,572.33 has been appropriated and paid to negro rural schools from the income of Anna T. Jeanes Fund, and $85,000 has been appropriated and paid to Spelman Seminary from the principal of the Laura S. Rockefeller Fund.

5. THE CARNEGIE FOUNDATION FOR THE ADVANCEMENT OF TEACHING.

Fundamental to Mr. Carnegie's doctrine of giving had been the idea that the purpose for which one gives must not have a degrading, pauperizing tendency upon the recipient.[25] To be able to give a pension and avoid such difficulties as these was the task Mr. Carnegie set for himself.

Believing that many evils were resulting from low salaries for professors and being familiar with the idea of teachers' pensions so widely practiced in

[25] The Gospel of Wealth, p. 21, ff.

Europe, Mr. Carnegie hoped to make the pension for the professor and his widow a regular part of the American educational system. He believed that if the teacher could receive his retiring allowance not as a charity but as a matter of right then pensions would raise the plane of academic life.[26]

Obviously, the income from the original gift of $10,000,000 would not meet the needs of the 700 or more institutions calling themselves colleges. First of all, therefore, the foundation was face to face with the question of what is a college. Secondly, having barred from participation in the fund all institutions under denominational control, the question of what constitutes denominational control must also be settled. The legal definition of a college which has been in operation in the State of New York furnished a basis for an answer to the first question,[27] and a definition of denominational college was arbitrarily decided upon and the foundation began operations, trusting to investigation and experience to clarify these definitions.

The first work of the foundation was to send out a circular asking all institutions of higher learning for information bearing upon: (a) The educational standards in use; (b) the relations of the school to the State, both in matters of control and support; (c) the relation of the school to religious denominations. In addition to this, information regarding salaries and size of faculties was asked for.[28] This brought together an unusually rich mass of educational data, which when digested by the foundation furnished the basis for its future action.

Out of this and succeeding studies came the quantitative definition of the college entrance "unit"; a clearer distinction between the work of a preparatory department and that of the college proper; as well as clearer conceptions of "college," of "State college," and of "denominational college." These accomplishments are pointed to here not only as an important contribution in standardization but also because of the wide discussion of these subjects which the action of the foundation provoked. Such work shows, too, how the foundation realized that in order to act wisely in the awarding of retiring allowances it must itself first of all become an "educational agency."[29]

This type of study is not the extent of the foundation's educational investigations. Its charter demanded that the trustees "do and perform all things necessary to encourage, uphold, and dignify the profession of the teacher and the cause of higher education."[30] In pursuance of this end the foundation has from the start undertaken to contribute liberally to the scientific study of higher education. In 1913 Mr. Carnegie added $1,250,000 to the endowment to meet the needs of a research department, and already the results of 11 extensive studies have been published and several others are under way. It is not possible to state accurately the value of this type of contribution. One might point to specific cases of more accurate university bookkeeping having resulted from the issuance of Bulletin No. 3, 1910, which presented 25 typical blank forms for the public reporting of the financial receipts and expenditures of universities and colleges; or to the revision of standards and the stir that was caused in the medical world by the issuance of Bulletin No. 4, 1910, describing the status of medical education in the United States and Canada; or to the legislative enactments following the recommendations made in Bulletin No. 7, 1907, giv-

---

[26] See The Policy of the Carnegie Foundation for the Advancement of Teaching, Educ. Rev., June, 1906.

[27] See First Annual Report of the President and of the Treasurer, p. 38.

[28] Ibid., p. 10, ff.

[29] See The Carnegie Foundation for the Advancement of Teaching. Second Annual Report of the President and Treasurer, p. 65.

[30] See quotation on p. 85.

ing the results of the survey of education in the State of Vermont; or to similar reactions to the reports dealing with engineering education and legal education, and in each instance show that the study brought direct results. The larger value of such work, however, can not be measured in that way. The sentiment for better medical schools which was created by the foundation's study has been a powerful factor in bringing about higher standards of training in that profession, and similar valuable results have come from other studies.

In administering the pension system the foundation has met with many difficulties, some of which have not been easy to overcome. From the outset the foundation has wisely dealt with institutions and not with individuals. It must not be said, however, that the foundation set itself up as a standardizing agency. It did set itself up as an educational agency, and very properly chose to administer its funds in terms of educational standards of its own choosing. In doing this no embarrassment was felt. The foundation named a list of "accepted institutions,"[31] explained why these were included, and no serious criticism of this list was offered by the public.

By the end of the first year the trustees stated that the questions of educational standards and of denominational or State control had been provisionally dealt with.[32] These questions continued to bring difficulties to the foundation, and for several years their reports show that they were exhaustively studied. The question of pensions for professors of State universities was solved in 1908 when Mr. Carnegie addressed a letter to the board in which he offered to add $5,000,000 to the endowment in order to meet that need.[33] Denominational colleges memorialized the trustees to modify their ruling affecting such institutions,[34] but with little success. Several sharp criticisms of the position of the foundation in this matter appeared in magazines,[35] but the trustees preferred to maintain their original standard.[36]

During the first few years the number of institutions eligible for the "accepted list" increased at an unexpected rate[37] and the foundation was compelled to revise its rules for granting pensions or otherwise plan to carry a heavier load. Within a very few years a number of colleges under denominational control, by proper legal process, had so modified their charters or articles of incorporation as to make them eligible to the accepted list,[38] the original actuarial figures had taken no account of the growth of the institutions,[39] and the number retiring under the "years of service" basis had been far greater than anticipated,[40] and other facts indicated that some modification of original

---

[31] The original list is printed in the foundation's first annual report above cited.
[32] See the foundation's first annual report above cited, p. 36 ff.
[33] See the foundation's third annual report, p. 62, for copy of his letter.
[34] See the foundation's fourth annual report, p. 4 ff.
[35] See letter by J. P. Cushing published in Nation, vol. 90, p. 233, and other articles in the same volume; also vol. 31 of Science.
[36] Carnegie Foundation for the Advancement of Teaching. Report, 1909, p. 6.
[37] Carnegie Foundation for the Advancement of Teaching. Report, 1909, p. 63.
[38] Bowdoin, Drury, Central University of Kentucky, and Drake University are illustrations.
[39] See the foundation's fourth annual report, p. 62.
[40] In his Review of Six Years of Administrative Experience the president of the foundation explains that the 25 years of service rule had been "adopted by the trustees under the assumption that but few applications would be made under it, and that these would be in the main applications from men who were disabled for further service. The intention was in fact to use the rule as a disability provision." "After a few years of administration it was perfectly clear that the rule was doing harm rather than good. It was therefore repealed by the trustees in accordance with the authority they had reserved in their hands," and was made a definite disability rule. See seventh annual report of the president and treasurer, 1912, p. 82.

plans would have to be made. At the outset the right to make such modification had been specially reserved,[41] partly upon the advice of actuarial experts. Accordingly, in 1909 the rules for granting retiring allowances were changed in two respects.

The original rules based the grant of a pension upon age or length of service in accordance with 10 specific rules. Rule 1 was revised to include instructors as well as the various grades of professors, deans, and presidents, and so really broadened the scope of the foundation's work to that extent. The original rules granting a pension after 25 years of service were changed so as to restrict such allowance to only such teachers as were proved by medical examination to be unfit for service. This latter change brought forth extensive criticism, raising the question of the ethical right of the foundation to do the thing it had specifically reserved the right to do, viz, to modify its rules " in such manner as experience may indicate as desirable."

The reasons for making these changes are more fully set forth in their 1904 report than it is possible to show in brief space. It serves our purpose here to note, first, that such change was made, and that the foundation was legally within its rights in so doing ; and, second, that the change met with strong opposition in many quarters.

There were slight modifications of these rules, but no important changes were proposed until the issuance to the trustees and to all teachers in associated institutions of the foundation's confidential communication in 1915, setting forth a Comprehensive Plan of Insurance and Annuities.[42] This communication called attention to the weak points in the existing system of pensions and proposed to replace the old system with a plan of insurance and annuities. More than 50 institutions complied with the request for criticism, and their statements are published in an appendix to the eleventh annual report of the foundation. Many faculties approved the plan in part, a few approved the plan in full as suggested, but altogether these statements, together with what appeared in the press, contain many important criticisms. It was argued, first, that the Carnegie Foundation had created certain expectations on the part of college teachers which it was morally obligated to fulfill ; second, that it is unjust to establish a system of insurance involving compulsory cooperation on the part of every teacher ; and, third, that commercial companies could offer a plan which would be financially more attractive.[43]

In 1916–17 the trustees passed a resolution referring the proposed new plan of insurance and annuities to a commission consisting of six trustees of the foundation, two representatives of the American Association of University Professors, and one representative each from the Association of American Universities, the National Association of State Universities, and the Association of American Colleges.[44] This commission agreed upon a plan of insurance

---

[41] See original Rules for Granting of Retiring Allowances in first annual report.

[42] This was later published as Bulletin No. 9 of the foundation.

[43] In the eleventh annual report of the president and treasurer President Pritchett virtually accepts the first of these objections as valid (see p. 24), and the trustees passed a resolution approving the idea of a contributory pension system which will operate " without unfairness to the just expectations of institutions or of individuals under the present rules." (See p. 4.) In the twelfth annual report a review of the year's work points out that the experience of 12 years' work has found the foundation " faced with two duties : First, to carry out fairly and to the best of their ability the obligations assumed in the associated institutions " ; and, secondly, to establish a system of insurance. Further the report says : " In the nature of the case the determination of what is a reasonable exercise of the power of revision retained by the trustees touches many personal interests." See pp. 19 and 30.

[44] Twelfth An. Rep. of the Foundation, 1916–17, p. 5, for the membership of this commission.

and annuities and recommended it to the trustees of the foundation.[45]   In May, 1917, it was voted to approve the fundamental principles of the teachers' pension system and also the combination of insurance and annuity benefits, as defined in the report of the above commission.[46]

This very soon led to the organization of the Teachers' Insurance and Annuity Association of America, chartered by the State of New York on March 4, 1918. This insurance company, together with a definite and fair plan for fulfilling the expectations of teachers who had belonged to the associated institutions under the original pension system, brought to a close what is likely to be regarded as the first period of the history of the Carnegie Foundation for the Advancement of Teaching. It was in many ways a stormy period in which sharp and often personal criticism was hurled at the foundation by individuals, through the press and even in the form of an investigation by the Federal Commission on Industrial Relations. Few direct replies to these criticisms have been made by the officers of the foundation except through the pages of their regular annual reports,[47] where every intelligent criticism has been dealt with.

It is obvious, even from this brief sketch of the history of this foundation, that what may be termed the elastic clause in its rules for granting pensions has been a most important one. The field was new and experience alone could point the way. Without the right to change its plans the foundation might have become a nuisance instead of a blessing. If that clause has given the foundation an easy way out of difficulties—too easy as some have thought—it has proved to be an excellent point of leverage for public opinion, and it must be evident to all that public opinion has not been ignored.

It must be said that the foundation has done some difficult pioneering in the field of teachers' pensions and has contributed liberally to the development and application of proper standards in the field of higher education. The following tables will give a partial financial view of the operations of the foundation up to June 30, 1917:

TABLE 39.—*Receipts and expenditures of Carnegie Foundation for Advancement of Teaching, 1906-1917.*[a]

Dates.	Total receipts.	Expenditures.				
		Retiring allowance.	Administration.	Publication.	Studies, etc.	Total.
1906 [b]	$292,673	....	$19,932	....	....	$19,932
1907	644,031	$158,890	39,906	....	....	198,797
1908	530,305	246,642	39,898	....	$531	287,072
1909	544,355	343,870	36,106	$7,983	9,494	397,455
1910	543,881	469,834	35,749	8,635	23,929	538,148
1911	590,449	526,879	36,743	9,414	7,406	580,443
1912	676,486	570,423	35,949	23,777	3,347	634,496
1913	694,195	600,390	36,632	3,579	....	640,601
1914	696,038	634,863	32,910	1,758	....	669,532
1915	712,852	674,724	36,550	1,576	....	712,852
1916	800,332	687,100	36,684	5,620	8	731,413
1917 [c]	625,862	547,358	33,772	6,390	2,461	625,862

a Compiled from the annual report of the treasurer of the foundation.   Cents are omitted.
b July 1 to Sept. 30.
c Oct. 1 to June 30.
[45] Ibid., appendix to Part II, for a full report of this commission.
[46] Ibid., p. 28 ff.
[47] President Henry S. Pritchett wrote a careful and dignified reply to such criticisms for the N. Amer. Rev. of April, 1915, " Should the Carnegie Foundation be Suppressed ; " and Secretary Clyde Furst gave an address before the Dept. of Sup., Nat. Ed. Assoc., in 1918, on " The Place of the Educational Foundation in American Education." This address was published in School and Society for March 30, 1918.

TABLE 40.—*Foundation's expenditures for allowances, each third year.*[1]

Years.	Institutions.		Retired teachers on roll.	Retiring allowances paid.	Widows' pensions.		Total amount paid.
	Kind.	Number.			Number.	Amount paid.	
1906 [2]...	Associated	52	44	$15,479	6	$1,125	$16,604
	Nonassociated	32	12	6,475	....	125	6,600
1908–9..	Associated	67	162	206,473	33	24,545	231,018
	Nonassociated	62	54	104,537	12	8,317	112,853
1911–12.	Associated	72	220	388,338	62	53,646	441,985
	Nonassociated	68	80	108,330	23	20,046	128,438
1914–15.	Associated	73	259	473,969	90	80,152	554,122
	Nonassociated	65	68	99,851	28	20,752	120,603
1916–17 [3]	Associated	71	274	345,214	112	116,891	462,105
	Nonassociated	64	62	62,054	32	23,199	85,253

[1] The amounts for the intervening years are not given, but approximate those here reported; see 12th An. Rep. of the foundation. Cents are omitted.
[2] From July 1 to Sept. 30.
[3] Oct. 1 to June 30.

6. THE RUSSELL SAGE FOUNDATION.

The Russell Sage Foundation has purposely avoided the field of higher education from the start,[48] but deserves mention here because of the contributions it has made to educational research.

Among its contributions are to be listed studies of retardation and elimination in city school systems, the medical inspection of schools, the care and training of crippled children, child-welfare work, health work in public schools, education through recreation, school buildings and equipment, and many other studies of direct or indirect value in reducing education to a science. Important, too, is the extensive work which the foundation has done in the field of educational surveys. The reports of the Springfield and the Cleveland surveys have aided materially in the establishment of standards for this kind of work. From the start the foundation's policy has been to spend its income on research and the dissemination of knowledge with a preventive intent. That it has carried out such a policy is evident to those who are familiar with its publications.

SUMMARY.

In this chapter it has been the purpose to describe the working principles and as far as possible to show the significance of our recently established philanthropic educational foundations. In form these foundations represent a new type of agency in educational philanthropy. In scope the possibility of service which they are empowered to render to higher education is almost without limit, and in the main each of the foundations occupies a field peculiarly its own.

These foundations are well characterized as attempts at reducing educational philanthropy to a business. The corporate principle is fully applied and the plan of administration is similar to that by which the affairs of a factory or a railroad are directed. In their most recent form the essential principles of a commission business are employed.

They are further characterized by the very general limitations placed upon the gifts by the founders; by the possibilities left open for reasonable changes in the original purpose, or even, in some cases, for a termination of the entire

[48] Schneider, Franz, jr. The Russell Sage Foundation, *in* Jour. Nat. Institute of So. Sciences, Dec. 20, 1915, p. 5.

trust; by the very careful plans devised for the administration of the funds; and by the entire absence of political, sectarian, or sectional control.

The work accomplished by these foundations can not be fully evaluated. In variety and extent it includes gifts and propaganda for the development of public schools, the endowment of colleges, fellowships, and pensions, as well as research in almost every field known to science. In all these fields their efforts have been fruitful.

The movement (for in the history of educational philanthropy it must be called a distinct movement) appears not yet to have reached its zenith. In character it is becoming more and more inclusive, and perhaps by that tendency may contribute to the establishment of the idea that education is but one of the many aspects of our social problem. The power which such institutions can turn toward the reconstruction of society has already been clearly indicated by the results described above, but quite as clearly has public opinion shown not only its ability to discern the possible misuses of that power but also its readiness to bring pressure to bear once a sign of such danger has been sensed. However much these foundations may supervise, therefore, and the promise in this respect is great, it is evident that they will themselves not go unsupervised.

Chapter VI.

SUMMARY AND CONCLUSIONS.

It has been the purpose of this study to inquire into the extent to which philanthropy has been responsible for the development of our institutions of higher learning, to discover what motives have prompted this philanthropy and how these motives have influenced college building, and, in addition, to try to bring to light whatever has been developed in the way of a theory of educational philanthropy and of educational endowments.

The study is covered in four chapters dealing, respectively, with: (1) The development of a theory of endowments and of philanthropy; (2) philanthropy of the colonial period; (3) philanthropy of the early national period, 1776–1865; (4) philanthropy of the late national period, 1865–1918; and (5) great educational foundations.

Various sources have been drawn upon, chief of which have been indicated by footnote references. These sources may be classified as having to do with what may be termed the qualitative and quantitative aspects of the problem, respectively. The former including charters, constitutions, by-laws, deeds of trust, wills, and other instruments of gift; the latter only with the bare figures and their analysis, or the statistics, of such gifts.

THE THEORY OF ENDOWMENTS.

At the beginning of college building in America there was no special theory of educational endowments or of educational philanthropy to work from. No careful thought had been given to the subject in England aside from discussions of practical situations, numbers of which were demanding attention long before America began to build colleges.

About the time Harvard College had reached its first centennial a really substantial discussion of the subject was entered upon in Europe and has continued practically ever since. The discussion was in connection with the general inquiry into the social institutions of the times, and represents one line of inquiry pursued by the new school of political economy just then taking form. Turgot, of France; Adam Smith, of England; and William von Humboldt, of Germany, were the chief early contributors in their respective countries and agree fairly well that education should not be endowed by the State, but rather that it should take its place in competition with all other interests. Turgot and Smith would modify the application of this laissez faire principle to meet certain conditions, while Humboldt would have it carried to its full

103

length. Doctor Chalmers, early in the nineteenth century, and John Stuart Mill, in 1833, however, proposed an important distinction between *need for food* and *need for education*, and urged that because of this difference the principle of free trade could not properly apply to education.

Owing to the bad state of educational endowments in England at that time, the discussion shifted somewhat to a consideration of the rights of the State in the control of endowments. The critics declared that the failure of these endowments was due to the very principles involved in endowments for education, while the Mill economists argued that it was due merely to failure of the State to exercise a proper control over them.

Other discussions in England of the possible value of endowments followed, involving the question of the right of posthumous disposition of property and emphasizing the rights of society (the State) as the real recipient of such gifts.

EARLY EXPERIENCES IN AMERICA.

In the early years America contributed little to this theoretical discussion, but as time went on and the idea of free public education began to take root, we gradually came face to face with it in connection with the question of school support. The State had taken a hand in initiating and in the support of our first attempt at higher education. The church had taken even a larger part than that shared by the State. In colonial Massachusetts, however, the State and the church were practically one, and therefore no opposition between the two was likely to appear. The church and the State in America were soon to rest upon the theory of complete separation, however, and then the question of responsibility for the support of schools had to be worked out. The building of colleges went on, the church, the State, and private philanthropy sharing the burden of cost, but with the responsibility for management resting mainly with the church until near the close of the colonial period.

At the beginning of the national period the State began to contribute less and less to the old foundations and to debate the question of State colleges or universities. By the middle of the new century the movement for State support and control of higher education took definite form. This did not rule out the church or private philanthropy, nor did it consciously interfere with them. It, nevertheless, set up competition between these two ideas of educational control. The result has been the development of a rather large literature on the subject, a decided stimulus to higher quality of work, and a clarification of the respective functions of the church and the State in higher education.

In the earlier decades private philanthropy was so completely dominated by the church on the one hand, and was so small and scattered on the other, that its place in the field of higher education had raised no serious questions. The development of State universities, however, brought criticism, and in more recent years such college buildings as that initiated by Ezra Cornell, Johns Hopkins, John D. Rockefeller, Leland Stanford, and Andrew Carnegie, and such nonteaching foundations as those discussed in Chapter V have raised the question of the possible good or ill that may come from State endowment and from private philanthropy on such a large scale.

It is in connection with these two points in our educational experience—the clash between State and church control; and the upsetting of the old and small practices by wealthy philanthropists through the launching of great competing universities, or by the establishment of vast funds for endowment, pensions, and investigation—that America's contribution to a theory of endowments or of educational philanthropy has been made. Writers on social and political theory have given the subject but little thought, though many legislative bodies have dwelt at length upon specific issues which have been raised by the clash of these forces.[1]

In colonial America the aim of higher education was from the start dominated by the general religious aim of the people, and whether the State and the church were one or not, it was almost without exception the church leaders who initiated the move for building a college, and the colleges of this period were primarily designed for the training of ministers.

The colonial governments of Massachusetts, Virginia, Connecticut, and New York contributed liberally to the maintenance of Harvard, William and Mary, Yale, and King's Colleges, respectively, but not so with Rhode Island, New Jersey, and New Hampshire in the case of Princeton, Brown, Dartmouth, and Rutgers. We are able to say, therefore, that philanthropy, motivated in the main by religion, was primarily responsible for initiating college building in all cases; that it was largely responsible for the maintenance of five of the nine colonial colleges, and almost solely so for the other four. We may say, too, that while the idea of State support for colleges was practiced, it was not common in all the Colonies, and in no case (William and Mary a possible exception) did a Colony assume full responsibility in the founding and development of a college. Hence denominational rather than State lines stand out in the history of higher learning in colonial times, and unless we think of the impetus given to " this worldly " education by Franklin in the beginnings of the University of Pennsylvania there was no experiment that could be called a real departure from the traditional idea of a college.

The sources from which philanthropy came during these years were numerous and varied, and each has in a way left its mark upon the college it benefited. No small amount of assistance came from England, largely through the influence of religious organizations. The influence of these gifts is suggested by the names of several of our colleges. Again, funds were sought in this country in Colonies quite remote from the college, and in many cases substantial aid was thus received. In the main, however, a college was either a local community or a denominational enterprise. If the former, as in case of Harvard, the burden rested mainly upon people close by. If the latter, as in the case of Brown, then churches of the denomination in question, wherever located, gave freely to its support. Many gifts from towns and from church congregations are also recorded.

One is impressed at every point with the very large number of small gifts and with the way in which they were obtained. This applies to the entire history of American college building. The thousands of small gifts to our colleges seem to record the fact that from the outset these were to be schools of the people.

During this period philanthropy initiated no unique educational experiments, yet it is quite as true to say that neither do we find evidence that gifts anywhere influenced education in a wrong way. Gifts which were made to some specific feature of a college went in the main to the library, to professorships, to scholarships, and to buildings, all of which are essential to any college. Throughout this period, however, it has been shown that a relatively large percentage of gifts were made to the college unconditionally.

We may say, then, that our beginnings were small; that they were warmly supported by the mother country; that the idea of State support was common, though by no means universal; that there is evidence that no State, with the possible partial exception noted, intended to assume full responsibility for the

---

[1] Note, for instance, the legislative debates in New York over the founding of Cornell University.

college; that philanthropy clearly did assume that responsibility; and that philanthropy did direct the policy of every college. We may say that philanthropy was motivated by religion, and that the church in most cases dominated the movement; that penury was common in all cases; that the thousands of small gifts constituted an important asset in that they popularized the idea of the college and so helped to democratize society; and that the gifts were in the main " to the college " without condition, or, if conditioned, they were almost invariably in accord with the essential lines of the school's growth.

THE EARLY NATIONAL PERIOD.

During the early national period there was no special break in the main forces that had been building colleges in the Colonies. Conditions under which these forces had to work, however, were vastly different, whether we think of the problems of State making, of religion, of industries, of exploration and settlement, of growth of population, or of social philosophy. It was an age of expansion in all these matters and that in a broad and deep sense.

In the matter of higher education it was also an age of expansion; expansion in numbers of colleges, and, to some extent at least, in educational aim and types of studies offered.

The Revolution had brought to an end the work of English philanthropy. and in increasing measure State support for established colleges was declining, leaving the task mainly to the churches of the country. The question of the State's function in higher education was soon raised, however, and before the close of the period a solution of the theoretical aspect of the problem had been reached and several State universities well established.

Whatever of promise there was in this new movement, however, the great college pioneering of this period was done almost entirely by church-directed philanthropy.

In this period, as in colonial days, the beginnings were small. Academies were often established with the hope that in time they would become colleges, the financial penury so common to the early colleges was characteristic throughout this period, and the subscription list was common everywhere.

The motive behind the work of the church was not only to spread the Gospel but to provide schools for the training of ministers to fill the increasing number of vacant pulpits reported throughout the period. Denominational lines were strong and undoubtedly led to an awkward distribution of colleges. The motives back of philanthropy in this period differ little therefore from those common to early Harvard, Yale, and Princeton. Among the older colleges, where the curriculum had begun to broaden and professional schools to take form, it was somewhat more common to find gifts made to some particular end. Among the newer foundations we see a fair duplication of the early history of the older colleges, except that the new colleges grew somewhat more rapidly. There is in most cases a more marked tendency to give toward permanent endowment, while among the conditional gifts those for professorships stand out strongly everywhere, and gifts to indigent students suffer a decline.

The development of professional schools, of the manual labor college, and of institutions for the higher education of women mark a change in our educational philosophy and give expression to the changing social life of the times. Most of these experiments were initiated and fostered by philanthropy.

Medical and law schools originated mainly as private schools conducted for profit, while schools of theology have been philanthropic enterprises from the start. The idea of women's colleges may have originated in the private pay schools for girls, or ladies' seminaries, common in the South, but the first well-financed college for women was the work of philanthropy, as most all subsequent attempts have been, and description of the work of philanthropy in these schools would fit fairly well any college of the period.

The fact that we find philanthropy rising to meet these many and varied educational and social ideas and ideals is not only an important fact in the social life of this country but is also an important characteristic of our educational philanthropy.

It is early in this period that the church education society comes into existence to answer the call of the church for more and better trained ministers. The work of these societies was extensive, and no doubt resulted in filling many vacant pulpits and church missions.

During this period, then, we may say that philanthropy did not slacken its interest in higher education, either because of the loss of English support or because of the rise of the State university. Philanthropy was, as before, directed in the main by the churches, and so through the whole period is prompted in the main by religious motives. The church college followed the westward-moving frontier, leaving many evidences of denominational competition for the new field. The failure of these church schools to meet the demands of the ministry is marked by the rise of church education societies whose aim was to provide scholarships and loans for students who would enter the ministry. Philanthropy was active in the movement toward separate professional schools, in the development of manual labor colleges, and in the origin and development of women's colleges during this period. These new enterprises may with some propriety be called educational experiments, credit for which must go to churches and to philanthropy.

As to method, there is practically nothing new to record. Permanent endowment grows somewhat more popular, and gifts for specified purposes tend to replace gifts to the general funds of the college. Nowhere, however, are the main aspects of the college neglected in favor of the new or unusual features.

THE LATE NATIONAL PERIOD.

After 1865 we enter a period of vast expansion in college building as in every other line. The idea of State higher education was worked out, and the question of State versus private and church schools was, for most people, satisfactorily solved. In the new States of the period it was more often the State than the church that established the pioneer institution for higher learning. With the exception of the manual labor college, practically all old ideas and practices in higher education were continued in force. Separate professional schools, women's colleges, church boards of education, and the typical small church college, all went forward, and each seems to have found a place for itself and still shows signs of healthful growth.

The period is equally well characterized by the development of new enterprises, back of which were at least a few really new things in educational philanthropy. One is the privately endowed university founded by a single large fortune. Another is the similarly endowed nonteaching educational foundation.

The more detailed description of the philanthropy of this period brought out the fact that among the old colonial foundations, as well as among colleges founded in the early national period, State aid was entirely lacking, while gifts were greatly increased both in numbers and size. It was noted that among the old colonial colleges the percentage of conditional gifts increased, while gifts to permanent funds showed a slight relative decline.

In the colleges of the early national period almost the opposite tendency was shown—rapid growth of permanent funds and rapid increase in gifts to the general fund. In all the colleges professorships, scholarships, and library were well remembered, though gifts to libraries among the older colleges did not grow so rapidly as was true in the younger schools. Everywhere it has been the fashion to give " to the college " outright or toward some main feature like buildings, equipment, library, professorships, or scholarships.

As compared with other kinds of philanthropy the data show that higher education is one of the greatest recipients of charity we have to-day, that a vast permanent endowment for higher education is being built up, and that philanthropy still bears the larger portion of the entire burden of cost. They bring out clearly the recent large movement of philanthropy toward the development of professional and technical schools and women's colleges, and also toward the larger support of church boards of education, the functions of which have been much enlarged in recent years.

GREAT EDUCATIONAL FOUNDATIONS.

During the last portion of the present period the great private foundation appeared as a form of educational philanthropy which was practically new. Each of these foundations represented the ideas and aspirations of the one man whose fortune gave it existence. Dominated by no church or religious creed, and not even by the man who established it, but only by public opinion and the corporation laws of State and Nation, these foundations have entered the educational field and left an impress on practically every type of educational enterprise in the country, whether private, State, or church.

The whole business and financial aspect of higher education has been studied and in a sense made over as a result of the operations of these gifts. The college curriculum has been more clearly differentiated from that of the secondary school, and standards of achievement in studies more clearly defined. Attention has been forcefully called to the problem of the distribution of colleges and to the principles which should guide us in locating new colleges. Millions have been added to the general endowment of higher education. Medical, legal, and engineering education have been enormously profited by the clear and impartial studies that have been made of these schools and by financial assistance. The scientific study of education has not only been greatly stimulated, but contributions have been made through experiments and investigation. The bounds of knowledge have been pushed out in many directions by extensive and costly research. The principles involved in pensions for teachers have been thoroughly studied from every angle and broadly and with some measure of satisfaction established.

Some doubts and fears and many sharp criticisms have been voiced lest these powerful corporations might seek to bias education and public opinion in favor of wrong social, political, or business ideals. This should be looked upon as a sign of health. Democratic society must not be expected to take such gifts on faith. Even if there is a grain of danger from such corporations, such danger should be mercilessly weeded out. In seeking for such dangers, however, we must not close our eyes to the obvious benefits which have and must continue to accrue to higher education from these sources. While society must insist upon its right to control such corporations, it must not be blind to the difficulties these foundations have had to face in blazing the new trails which they respectively have chosen to mark out in the field of higher education. If the church, the State, the university, the professor, and the general public will continue to distinguish between intelligent criticism, on the one hand, and mere suspicion and gossip on the other, and remember that a wise administration of these gifts is largely dependent upon a cooperating and appreciative beneficiary, then this, the greatest experiment in educational philanthropy that has ever been tried, will continue to prove its worth to society.

DEVELOPMENTS BEARING UPON A THEORY OF ENDOWMENTS.

From all this giving, what have we learned about the meaning of philanthropy itself? What attitude shall the State, the church, and society in general take toward the great stream of gifts that is continuously pouring into the lap of higher education in the country?

It is obvious that gifts to colleges are accepted by all as great blessings, and practically nowhere is there evidence that people fear the power which may some day be exercised through these gifts; that is how firmly the college has established itself in the confidence of the people. So many thousands of people have contributed small or large gifts to build these schools, so closely have the schools been associated with the church, and so intimately have they woven themselves into the life of the people that they are everywhere fully trusted, and thus far no very bad effects of philanthropy have been felt.[2] Even the great privately endowed institutions like Cornell (accepted with much misgiving at the outset in many quarters) have now fully won the confidence of the people in general, of the church, and of the State. This is not surprising in the light of the study of the conditions placed upon the thousands of gifts classified in the course of this study.

If there is any misgiving in the minds of the people about any educational philanthropy to-day, it is perhaps in reference to one or another of the recently established nonteaching foundations. Here some uncertainty exists, as has been pointed out, though even here there is comparatively little that has not been accepted in most quarters with full confidence.

If philanthropy has so nearly won the entire confidence of the people, it is because of the record philanthropy has made for itself. In defining the meaning of education, or in setting the limits to its participation in college building, donors have not departed too far from the accepted ideas, ideals, and practices of the time and of the people they sought to serve. Millions have been given for permanent endowment but the practice has been to endow " the college," a " professorship," a " scholarship," a given line of " research," a " library," and rarely or never to define with any severe detail just what is to be included under the term " college," " professorship," " scholarship," etc. The result is that the writer has found little evidence of harmful or even useless foundations, large or small.

In the light of these facts it seems fair to assume that the great dominating motive in educational philanthropy has been desire to serve society; or, if we prefer, desire for a very high type of notoriety. So far as social progress is concerned, these are but two views of the same thing.

---

[2] The writer did not find it feasible in this study to inquire into the number of gifts that have really laid a burden upon the college. In his autobiography, President White, of Cornell, expresses the opinion that our colleges have too frequently been the recipients of such gifts as an observatory, leaving the college the responsibility of purchasing instruments and caring for upkeep.

It has been pointed out that most that has been done toward developing a theory of educational philanthropy in this country has grown directly out of the practice rather than out of the studies of social and political theory. The country has faced and solved certain fundamental questions as they have arisen, as: The function of the State in higher education; the function of the church in higher education; the function of private philanthropy in teaching and non-teaching activities touching higher education. In settling these questions there has been endless debate and some bitterness of feeling, yet we have fully accepted the idea of State-endowed higher education, and, according to our practice, defined that education in the broadest possible way. This acceptance of State-endowed education did not rule out the church, whose activities in college building are as much appreciated and as well supported as ever. That there should have been a clash between the old idea of church-directed education and the new idea of State education was to be expected. The outcome of such a clash in this country, however, could not have been different from what it was. Similarly, there was a clash between the church and the privately endowed types of colleges, but each has a well-established place in present practice.

In this country we have not confined ourselves to any single notion about who shall bear the burden of higher education. The State establishes a university but it also encourages the work of the church and of private philanthropy.[3] The practice is therefore based upon a theory that is not fully in line with those of the early English, French, and German philosophers. It is far more liberal, being based rather upon the underlying conceptions of our social and political organization.

Ownership of property in this country carries with it the right of bequest, and the " dead hand " rests, in some degree, upon most of the institutions of higher education. We fully respect the rights and the expressed wishes of the educational benefactors,[4] but this study shows that the benefactors have also respected the rights of society, not the society of to-day only but that of future generations as well. There has been a growing tendency for colleges and universities to study the terms of proffered benefactions with utmost care and to refuse to accept gifts to which undesirable conditions are attached. Similarly there has been a growing tendency on the part of benefactors either to accept terms suggested by the institution or to make the gift practically without conditions or with specific provision for future revision of the conditions named. This, it seems to the writer, marks an achievement which guarantees society against most if not all the evils associated with endowed education.

After an examination of the hundreds of documents which have furnished the basis of this study, the writer is inclined to look upon educational philanthropy as an essential and highly important characteristic of democracy.

If a statement were made of the theory which has been evolved or the principles which have been arrived at in the almost three centuries of practice, they would seem to be about as follows:

(1) Permanent endowment of higher education by the State, by the church, or other association, or by individuals, is desirable.

(2) All gifts to education, whether for present use or for permanent endowment, whether large or small, should be encouraged, because they open

---

[3] Usually the property of such schools is made entirely, or at least in part, free from taxation by State laws.
[4] As note the Girard College case.

up large possibilities in the way of educational investigation and experiment and because the donor is brought into an intimate relationship with an enterprise that is fundamental to the national life.

(3) The wishes of a donor as expressed in the conditions of his gift shall be respected and fully protected by the State.

(4) It is desirable that the conditions controlling a gift shall be stated in general terms only, and that the methods of carrying out the purposes of the donor be left largely to the recipient of the gift.

(5) Finally, it is desirable that even the purpose of a gift should be made alterable after a reasonable period of time has elapsed, and, if it be desirable, that the gift be terminated.

INDEX.